RIVI

MW00647795

Published by Mission Point Press
2554 Chandler Rd.
Traverse City, MI 49696
(231) 421-9513
www.MissionPointPress.com

Cover Design Layout: Donna Montgomery,
DMZ Designs, Traverse City, MI

ISBN: 978-1-950659-64-7

Library of Congress Control Number: 2020910632

Printed in the United States of America

River Love

The true story of a wayward Sheltie, a woman, and a magical place called Rivershire

Tricia Frey

Mission Point Press

For Sheldon

Sheldon and Tricia, August 2010,
Rivershire. BARBIE STERLING

Contents

Foreword

Her essence shines through when she tends her gardens and cares for her animals at a unique and special piece of Planet Earth's Garden in Northwest Michigan called Rivershire.

She is my sister, Tricia, who, in 2005, joined me in acquiring a wooded, riverside property— full of promise, but in need of some tender loving care. Calling this place home, Tricia entered into an unspoken arrangement with the river property, each providing to the other the love and nurturance needed to flourish, grow, and trust.

At the center of this story is attraction; a sacred place that draws fractured beings in and offers time and space for healing. The wonder of the night sky, the reassuring warmth of the sun, the songs of the pines and their inhabitants, the ever-changing constant of the river beckons one to rest awhile, to be still, to know.

Many have been attracted to this sacred place: people, cats, dogs, and even a seemingly genteel black bear. Most passed through, but a few remained to dwell for a time. All left behind valuable lessons on life and love. And through it all Tricia has been a constant, attending to life forms transitory and permanent. As caretaker, steward, and mother, her resonance with Rivershire is part of its peacefulness, its beauty, its magic. Like the river and verdant surroundings, her presence will remain long after she has moved on.

In essence, this book is about living, loving, and parting at a place that attracts the injured; it affords healing to those who are worthy and expels those who are not. And it is also about the doggie that runs through it; his adventures, the friends made along the way, the love shared, the lessons left in his wake. Sheldon, the Amaizin' Blue Wonder Dog. He will not only touch your heart— he will mend it, one stitch at a time.

May you sense the peace, beauty, and magic of Rivershire in the telling of this story.

With gratitude and love,
Sandra

Author's Note

The story you are about to read is true. I've been careful when sharing details about the lives of others, either conscientiously guarding their privacy or choosing not to include that which doesn't honor the story. I'm rather protective of this tale, which means so much to me; what I reveal about myself does not concern me. What I reveal about others does. Sheldon is as authentic a creature as has ever lived and does not care what I share about him. With nothing to hide, Sheldon always remained true to his character and spirit. Oh, to live life like a dog.

—*Tricia Frey*

BARBIE STERLING

I learned a long time ago if you give your heart to a pet, you're bound to have it broken. I learned a lot later how much the heartache is worth. —TF

WILLIAM J. SAGE

Prologue

With that first rumble of thunder, I sit straight up in bed out of a dead sleep.

"Damn it. He's going to run again."

Sheldon has been running ever since I've known him. Running from thunder, running from me, or running from fear—it's hard to know.

I do my own share of running, too. Well, not literally. I'd rather walk. However, in my metaphorical running I prefer to head toward shelter, not away from it. Gimme shelter. Oh yes, please do.

Not Sheldon. Shelter awaits, but he wants nothing to do with it.

I lie back down and say a prayer while a tear slips from my eye. I wonder if Mary, in her bed next door, is doing the same. Probably. We tend to shed a few tears for Sheldon during thunderstorms.

"Please keep him safe. Please bring him back. Please help me get him inside this house. Please let him trust me. Let him know he can." Eventually, I fall asleep again.

Life Begins
at the River

I first saw the Sheltie dog that I eventually named Sheldon on an average day in the early spring of 2006. I lived then (and still do) at a place we call Rivershire, on the Boardman River just south of Traverse City, Michigan. My sister Sandra and I purchased the property in the summer of 2005, taking possession in mid-August. Joined by our sister Becki, who lived nearby in Traverse City with her long-time boyfriend Ronnie, we celebrated that day by standing in the river with a bottle of champagne, toasting to our purchase and new endeavor.

The land is extraordinary in natural beauty, home to sturdy hardwoods and towering pines. The river curves around the property, offering river views and access on the south, west, and north. The size and positioning of the property provides privacy while still being manageable. At the time of our toasting the swift-flowing river ran clear and pristine, deep enough to offer the opportunity for canoeing and kayaking, yet shallow enough for wading.

The Boardman River is rife with history, which I am ill-equipped to relate in detail. It is documented that Hemingway fished her waters, but I will leave those accounts to the qualified historians. For my humble purposes, I am delighted by the mere thought that the great Ernest may once have fished from the banks of Rivershire.

Across the river is a steep bank, with a railroad track running near the top of the rise. A natural spring issues from the bank into the river. The river and spring flow continuously, never freezing even on the bitterest of cold winter days, and the constant sound of running water adds a calming, soothing aura to the already-tranquil atmosphere. A train, pulling just six freight cars at most on its most ambitious runs, occasionally passes by. When it does, it will pass by again that same day, heading in the opposite direction to return back where it came from. This train is part of the charm of the place. It has always seemed to me as though Rivershire came with its own life-sized Lionel train set, provided simply for our amusement. It is one of two sources of traffic off the front porch.

The second source involves kayaks, canoes, and inner tubes carrying inhabitants enjoying a river float. For a property twelve miles south of downtown Traverse City, there is, between the train track and the river (which often replicates a liquid sidewalk), a fair amount of passer-by activity.

Folks pass by during every season and on any given day—the occasion of our toasting and rejoicing was no exception. As we stood in the river, members of a self-appointed Boardman River clean-up committee floated by. These dedicated lovers of the Boardman were the first river travelers we met, and their appearance was perfectly timed. Meeting others who loved the river enough to spend time caring for it set a tone for the day, enhancing the excitement and affection for the river we were already feeling. It was inspiring. The river took them by at a leisurely pace, allowing us to share a brief conversation (and some of our champagne). Those who had passed by before realizing there was bubbly being shared back-paddled and returned for a sip or two. We christened our lives on—and love of—the Boardman River that day.

Rivershire is a magical place. One can almost see the gnomes, fairies, and nymphs resting in the tree branches, peeking from among the rocks, and frolicking in the shade of the flora. That land lured us in and at the time of our arrival, we had nary an inkling how its wonder and powers would change all our lives in significant ways in the years to come. That same power of attraction is what brought Sheldon to Rivershire. The pull was not of our making: call it divine intervention, the aligning of the planets, or simple fate. I have no exact word or phrase. None of us could have avoided the pull had we tried. We were metal, and Rivershire was our magnet.

It would take years—and the substantial proof of

many transformative experiences—for me to comprehend Rivershire's true mystical nature. What was, however, initially and clearly evident to both Sandra and me, was the Tolkien-like quality of the place and we wanted its name to reflect such character. In our pondering, the word shire presented itself and the connection was made. Rivershire eventually became synonymous with healing, transformation, enlightenment, safe harbor, and even redemption to us. A haven, a refuge, a home.

Home

Although we took possession in August, I didn't move to Rivershire until November. Sandra, who lives in Ohio, purchased Rivershire as a vacation home and investment opportunity. A quaint and rustic cabin across the driveway from the main house gives Sandra her own accommodations when visiting, providing the perfect scenario for dual ownership: separate dwellings, with space for gathering or parting ways as desired.

The main house is divided into two sides, with a shared garage in the center. One half is my home; the other half serves as an apartment, housing a variety of occupants over the years. Two in particular are significant to this story, starting with our sister Mary. She moved up from Ohio in the summer of 2006, after her marriage of forty years ended in divorce.

During the months that passed from the christening in the river to the day I settled in, a great remodeling took place. We took possession of

Rivershire knowing this was inevitable, but, as these projects go, we had no idea of the scope and scale. Our efforts produced a charming two-sided dwelling.

I thought I was beating the winter weather by scheduling the move for November 18. That day, the northern Michigan lake effect snow machine mimicked the date by providing 18 inches of snow. Moving in was difficult and miserable, but we persevered.

Upon reflection, moving day was its own forecast. Our future at Rivershire—in spite of being piloted there by universal, unavoidable forces—would, along with joys, triumphs, and life-affirming moments, douse us with turmoil, trouble, and heartbreak, too. In other words, Rivershire is a home, just like any other.

I Call Him Sheldon

In the early months of 2006 I settled into Rivershire, as did my two cats, Snickers and Gracie. Snickers had been my cat for ten years, and Gracie, who I adopted as a kitten, was about five years old. Snickers came into my life in 1996 when my husband (at the time) brought her home one cold winter's night. When he and I separated a few months later, I took Snickers with me to my new apartment, and we began developing what would become a close connection. Well-behaved, fun, and loving, Snickers could have been a poster cat for superb feline behavior.

Gracie, on the other hand, would not have made the poster. She could be sweet: intuitive and caring one minute, lying across my chest with a paw on each shoulder while lavishing me with kitty kisses when I needed them most. However, her demeanor could change to psycho-kitty in a split second, causing her to turn on me or any creature she deemed unworthy of being in her presence. Her mission in life was to torment Snickers by chasing and cornering her, leaving Snickers traumatized. Gracie exhibited every form of bad behavior, including habitual peeing on couches, rugs, and blankets. I'd tried to love the crazy out of her and hoped Rivershire would have a calming effect.

One day, as I sat relaxing on the couch, I noticed something move outside the front window. I rose and saw a medium-sized dog with contrasting gray, black, and white fur. His head snapped up when he saw me through the window. Our eyes locked but just for a moment. Then he turned and took off like a shot, running for the property next door. I moved pretty fast myself, scampering over to the kitchen window to see where he went. "Yep," I said aloud to no one in particular (unless the cats were listening), "that must be the neighbor's dog. He knows he's not supposed to be over here."

But I was wrong. As days, weeks, and months passed, I continued to see him occasionally. He lurked around my yard and in the small scrub of woods near my driveway. I didn't yet know he was male, but as I watched him I saw that he lifted his leg to pee, so I assumed as much.

I concluded he was a stray even though he was wearing a red collar. He must have belonged to someone at some point. I couldn't tell if there were any tags on the collar. I called to him, trying to coax him to come to me, but he was terrified and incredibly skittish. I brought him food and treats, but he didn't come close enough to accept them from me directly. I would place treats on the ground and gingerly step back. When he determined I had moved far enough away, he ventured forward to accept the tasty morsels, retreating to the safe zone of the scrub before eating them.

Spring morphed into summer, and Mary moved north to become the first resident of Rivershire's apartment. Mary had lived in our small Ohio hometown all her life. With her marriage over and her children raised and on their own, it was the perfect time for a change of scenery.

I was no longer the sole human living full-time at Rivershire. At first, I didn't know if it would work having sisters sharing space on the same property, even one that offered a home divided into separate living quarters (for Mary and me) and a cozy cabin for Sandra's occasional escapes north. Rivershire, however, knew better than I, providing us with a beautiful scenario that included closeness and space, interaction and solitude.

Mary, Sandra, Becki, and I are four of nine children—all individual births, no twins, no triplets. I am the youngest. Becki is the next oldest to me, and Sandra is the next oldest to Becki. Mary is number five—smack dab in the middle. There was a theme of three where the Frey kids were concerned. My parents first had three boys—Bob, Ron, and Butch. Then, they had three girls—Suz, Mary, and Jane. Those first six children were born within a period of seven years, eight months. Four-and-a-half years after Jane was born, Sandra came along followed by Becki and me, with the last three of us spaced out over the next nine years. My parents moved three times in their married life, and each new home brought three more children. My dad often said, "Every time we moved we had three more kids, so we finally stopped moving!"

The week I was born, my oldest brother—who was 21 at the time—moved out west. He stopped at the hospital as he was leaving town to say hello to me and goodbye to Mom. We were raised in a Mennonite home and always lived in the country. The final stop was an 80-acre farm outside of Archbold, Ohio. We lived in a two-story brick farmhouse, with little or no heat upstairs. Cold winters meant piles and piles of quilts on top of piles and piles of kids. There was a large, beautiful barn on our farm and (eventually) two ponds on the property. By the time I was five, I became an aunt for the first time. My niece Lori—Mary's daughter and my parents' oldest grandchild—and I were and remain very close, not only in age, but in love and friendship.

Even though Mary, Sandra, Becki, and I had been biological sisters for a long time, a true sisterhood began at Rivershire. We were each making a fresh start. Mary was moving forward after her divorce with a new home, job, and friends. Sandra's husband of thirty years had passed away from esophageal cancer three years earlier, and she was learning to live her life without him. Becki and Ronnie got married in my living room at Rivershire just one week after I moved in: based on previous experience, each had wondered if they would ever wed again. Finding what they needed in each other, they took that brave step at Rivershire in the glow of sparkling lights Ronnie draped across a lush pine tree just outside the living room window.

As for me, I needed the move to Rivershire more than I could possibly imagine at the time. I possessed a smoldering discontent deep within, of which I was only mildly aware and ill-equipped to clarify and heal. I ignored the unidentified dullness inside of me by scurrying though my days, looking for my next distraction, my next refuge. To assuage any critical voice I stayed busy, made friends, and had fun, settling into a routine that offered little in the way of self-exploration. Instead, I constructed a cocoon in which I could safely and comfortably reside. The silk I spun around myself provided shelter from an agony I did not clearly recognize, let alone care to embrace.

When the prospect of purchasing the river property with Sandra went from a fun idea to the final process of either signing the papers or walking away, I was terrified. I sensed that such a move would rip me from my state of comfortable oblivion. It came down to me to decide if we were moving forward with the purchase. Sandra was ready, was I?

I said yes for two reasons. One, I adored the idea of living on the river. I had long dreamed of residing by a northern Michigan body of water, and here was my chance! Two, I didn't want to disappoint Sandra. She never once indicated my refusal would disappoint her, simply wanting confirmation that we were both fully on board and ready to accept our respective responsibilities. It was only in my brain that I equated saying no with letting her down.

I needn't have agonized, for the decision was truly not mine to make. Over the years we would witness many wonders of Rivershire's devising, not least of which was our arrival in our new sanctuary. Our pilgrimage there was nothing short of miraculous, predestined many years before by life events that otherwise would be unconnected and, for Sandra, involved personal loss and heartbreak.

Sandra began visiting Becki and me in Traverse City frequently after her husband Stace passed away in 2003. Theirs was a love focused on mutual respect and understanding, with shared passions, open communication, and a beautiful balance of independence and togetherness. Sandra felt Stace's absence very deeply. Coming north provided Sandra space in which she could commune with us and nature, helping her to process her grief.

After a couple years of such visits, Sandra expressed her possible interest in purchasing land in northern Michigan, but there were specifics involved. They included waterfront property of some form or another, a good investment, and a sense of sanctuary. Her biggest concern was property maintenance and security, since she lived over four hours away. After giving this all some thought, I proposed the possibility of dual ownership. If the right opportunity came along, I could sell my house and live on-site to provide property management and oversight. We agreed this was something to consider.

Within weeks of our conversation, while I was visiting Sandra in Ohio in early April 2005, Becki called to tell us a beautiful property along the Boardman River had just gone up for sale. There was an open house being held that very day: Becki and Ronnie only heard about it because the property was owned by dear, longtime friends of Ronnie's family. Ronnie himself spent much time there as a boy, *rump-bumping* as they called it over rocks as they floated in inner tubes down the flowing waters of the Boardman. The property had been in the same family for decades. That it was up for sale, instead of being passed along to the next generation, was surprising to many—a rare and unforeseen opportunity.

Becki and Ronnie attended the open house, mindful of Sandra's criteria. Waterfront? Check! Good investment? Seemed likely. A sense of sanctuary? Without a doubt. Available space to offer a year-round dwelling for me plus getaway space for Sandra? Absolutely. It seemed a more perfect scenario could not possibly exist.

Four months later, we took possession of our slice of paradise.

Each of us in the Rivershire Sisterhood was evolving, experiencing our metamorphosis both separately and together thanks to a special place we all came to revere. The four of us started forming a bond we had never before experienced, one born of circumstance, need, and opportunity.

For Mary and me, life at the river eased into daily routines, enhanced by the occasional sighting of one skittish Sheltie. One day Mary wanted to know, "Tricia, have you seen that dog out there?"

"Indeed I have. I call him Sheldon."

Building Sheldon's House

If we were going to have a dog living at Rivershire, even as an occasional resident, he would need a house. Mary and I decided to upgrade a rickety old shed on the property into a doggie condo. We headed to a home improvement store for the necessary supplies, and as we strolled inside I became a little giddy. "Okay," I told Mary. "We'll haggle a bit. We'll tell them about Sheldon and maybe they'll even donate the stuff we need." We were determined to get a good deal. After all, we were about to construct a home for a wayward dog with no idea if the skittish little guy would even go inside. Keeping our costs to a minimum was important.

We went in armed with a list. Insulation, both the fiberglass and blue board varieties, was required. We also needed a piece of plywood, some glue, and a large, heavy-duty tarp. We found an associate. We told our story. We wheeled. And dealed. We got a

discount on broken pieces of insulation, yet somehow we still managed to spend over $100.

The prospective resident of the soon-to-be-re-
modeled shed was lurking in the scrub when we
arrived home. As though he was our project super-
visor, Sheldon settled in a short distance away and
watched our efforts with great interest.

The metal shed was the color of putty and shaped
like an outhouse, with a pitched roof and a narrow,
sliding door. It was a piece of junk. Next to the
door were the letters *i* and *T*, stacked. For whatever reason, the *i* was lowercase, the *T* capitalized.
Every time I looked at the shed I wondered if it
ever had been an outhouse, even though it was certainly no longer perched over an open, smelly pit.
I thought those letters next to the door may have
been previously preceded by two more letters—*S*
and *h*—to indicate at least one of the things people
may want to do while inside. Perhaps the *S* and *h*
fell off, or they only existed in my warped imagina-
tion, but it instantly became the Shit-Shed to me.
An old metal shack, basically discarded but still
standing—it remained for a reason and was about
to have purpose once again.

We unloaded the car and approached the Shit-
Shed. The metal door made a horrible screeching
sound when I pulled it open.

"Okay, Mary, I'm going in. If there's a snake or
huge spider in here, you'll know it."

Inside I found an empty, stark interior, eight
feet or so in height. The shed was narrow, and I
could easily touch all four walls. "First thing we

need to do is install some insulation," I explained to Mary. "Then we can add the drop ceiling. That way Sheldon will be able to stay warmer by conserving his body heat. We want the heat he naturally produces to stay contained to help keep him warm."

As I spoke about body heat, I felt it. Something was crawling on my neck. Shrieking ensued, accompanied by hands slapping and arms flailing. Plenty of flailing. I fled the space, still shrieking, slapping, and flailing. "IS THERE A SPIDER ON ME?!?! IS THERE A SPIDER ON ME?!?!"

"I'm sure if there was it's long gone now," Mary said. "Hold still. I don't see anything. You are not right." That is a good way to describe me in full-blown spider phobia mode—not right.

After calming down I returned to the shed, and Mary joined me. We squeezed ourselves in there together and got to work. It was a tight fit.

The first step involved wedging insulation into place and adhering it to the metal walls using a combination of heavy-duty construction glue and spray foam insulation. Next came installation of the drop ceiling, supported by an old kayak oar wedged diagonally across the shed. The ceiling itself was made of layers of insulation, perfectly cut to fill the area, allowing no cold air to flow downward from the shed's top half.

We stepped outside and filled the base with fiberglass insulation. On top of that we placed the piece of plywood, which was supported by a metal lip that ran around the shed's interior at the bottom. While it may not have held a full-grown man, it would certainly hold Sheldon, whom we estimated weighed around fifteen to twenty pounds.

We topped the floor with blue board insulation and a carpet remnant left over from the remodeling project at Rivershire. The Shit-Shed had wall-to-wall carpeting! We laid an old blanket down, along with four large pillows that were no longer of any use to me but would provide Sheldon with warm, cushy comfort. Lastly, we added a big comforter that I got from the Goodwill store for four bucks.

With our interior project complete, we moved on to the exterior.

First, we draped the tarp over the shed, staking all four corners securely to the ground for optimum protection from wind and rain. With the shed's door slid halfway shut and insulation wedged firmly in the upper gap of the doorjamb, there remained a perfectly sized doggie door at the base. The tarp hung just low enough to serve as a door flap.

The final step of our makeshift building project was to add the pièce de résistance: an old, weathered picnic table, handmade by a true woodworking artisan. It was, literally, on its last leg. The table had been relocated many times, dragged from Michigan to Ohio and back to Michigan again. It was beautifully crafted and deserved better treatment. However, this special table was being granted a new life as gateway protector of Sheldon's home, warding off wind and weather from entering the only portal.

As we stood the table on its end I saw the message

etched into its underside, inscribed there many years before by its maker. *May those who gather at this table feel forever surrounded by love.* I wished for that and more on Sheldon's behalf.

The table's seven-foot length jutted into the sky. It was somewhat supported by its one remaining leg, which would not provide enough stability against a strong wind gust. We found a discarded metal post stashed away in the pole barn and wedged it—we got damn good at wedging stuff—into the ground at such an angle as to securely support the table. The wind block for the doorway was solid, ready to protect its domain and precious inhabitant like a wooden sentinel.

Sweating profusely and covered in dirt, insulation, and whatever else fell on us from the inside of that ancient metallic outhouse-shaped shed, we stepped back to survey our handiwork. I remained convinced that a spider the size of a small country had taken up purchase somewhere on me, probably in my hair. "Sheldon, I hope you use this little hut of yours. I don't risk getting chomped by a wolf spider for just anyone, you know. You must be pretty special."

We didn't know if Sheldon would move in, but we knew one thing for sure. We were ready for a drink. We mixed a couple of cocktails and settled in on Mary's porch to watch and wait.

Sheldon observed the entire process as we transformed the i.T. house into an inhabitable dwelling. He watched me flail about and holler like a crazed lunatic. We questioned whether he would go inside, but we didn't have to wait long for an answer. In the same amount of time it took me to ask Mary, "Are you ready for another one?," Sheldon approached his new custom-made abode. He looked at i.T. He looked at us. Then, he strolled inside to check out his new digs. Our labor of love had been accepted.

Sheldon had a home, and we had a dog.

Getting
to Know
Sheldon

Days stretched into weeks, weeks into months. We made Sheldon's acquaintance any way we could, completely on his terms. Even though he wouldn't come near enough for us to touch him, he simply could not resist the tantalizing wonder of that glorious outdoor device called a grill. Every cookout, party, or simple grilled dinner provided a reason for Sheldon to come closer—but not too close—and wait, oh so patiently, as the grilling commenced. Sheldon understood that when we cooked outside, good things were bound to happen. When we grilled burgers, we made a small one for Sheldon. If chicken was on the menu, a doggie-sized portion was provided. During each grilling session Sheldon inched a bit closer, sensing a delightful enticement, knowing from experience that bravery was rewarded and, so far, no harm had come his way from this form of courage.

Sheldon received more than his share of hot dogs during parties at Rivershire. Guests were intrigued by this timid, adorable creature and, naturally, they wanted to feed the little guy. Consequently, wieners were tossed his way—lots and lots of wieners. I knew this not only from what I witnessed, but by the dozens of buried hot dogs I unearthed while gardening. Sheldon had become accustomed to living in survival mode, so when more food was offered than he could consume, he instinctively buried the excess for another day. He hadn't fully grasped that food and shelter would always be provided so long as he stayed at Rivershire. What he *had* fully grasped was that he liked hot dogs more than the dry food we provided for him daily. Wieners ruled.

But what ruled more than anything to which the common wiener could possibly aspire was the simple yet incredibly tasty pork steak. Every time I grilled a pork steak, it was a special occasion in Sheldon's world. When the meat was done I cut out the bone, leaving a decent amount of pork attached, and, as soon as it was cool enough, I held it out for Sheldon's taking. This became an important ritual in our trust development. He had gotten quite brave, and when I reached out with pork steak bone in hand, he inched forward just close enough to gently snatch it from my fingers and dart off for the perceived safety of the scrub by his house. I would watch from afar as he held the bone between his front paws and gnawed upon his favorite of all treats. Sheldon and I began a communion of sorts around the grill, one pork steak at a time.

The grill was not the only vehicle of culinary delight for Sheldon. At the time he and I were becoming acquainted, I was working a busy weekend schedule as a wedding DJ. Most of my Saturday summer nights were consumed with hours of spinning love songs, dance classics, booty jams, and hip-hop. Fortunately for Sheldon these nights were also filled with plenty of food, much of which went back to the kitchen uneaten, often untouched.

One night, when I slipped into the catering kitchen to return my dinner plate before the cake-cutting and couple's first dance, I watched as a server scraped beautiful pieces of prime rib and chicken breast into the trash.

"Stop!" I shrieked. "I have a stray dog at home. Can we scrape that into some containers? I'd love to take it home for him."

She gave me a questioning look. I quickly added, "I swear it's not for me. There really is a stray at my house. His name is Sheldon, and he would love that meat."

With that, a Saturday night ritual began.

The first evening I came home with boxes full of wedding delicacies, I stopped in the driveway near Sheldon's house. When I called to him he came right out and, while keeping his distance, watched me carefully to see what I might be up to. I tore the top off one of the polystyrene carryout boxes, placed a few tender, juicy bites of prime rib on the lid, and set the makeshift doggie dish on the ground. "Here you go, buddy. I had a wedding tonight and brought you some special treats."

Sheldon crept up to the plate, snatched a tender morsel, then turned and trotted off to a safe spot near his hut. Let the feasting begin. He was eating like a king, or, more accurately, like a groom.

For the next few days pieces of prime rib and chicken were tucked inside his dry food bowl. Next Saturday, the caterers included some fish in the take. I found out rather quickly that fish was not Sheldon's protein of choice. He looked at me with an expression that seemed to say, "Do I look like a cat to you?" No buddy, you do not.

So beef and chicken it was. Sheldon, being a very smart dog, always seemed to know when it was Saturday night. Arriving home between midnight and 2:00 a.m., I would find him lying near the driveway, on the lookout for me and the wedding booty. It was uncanny; Sheldon patiently waiting for me to stop and deliver the goods, like a doggie drug drop, and him ready for his fix.

Aside from grilled meats and wedding treats, table scraps were often mixed in Sheldon's bowl of dry food to encourage kibble consumption. Mary and I soon discovered Sheldon was not a fan of the pea. If the scraps contained peas, they were avoided with expert proficiency. Every bite of dinner vanished except for the lowly pea. Why a creature—who had basically been starving out in the wilderness, presumably eating anything from dead animals to the fecal matter of living ones—would take the time to meticulously lick around the smallest vegetable known to man was beyond this woman.

We started off feeding Sheldon by his house, gradually moving his bowl closer until it finally found its way onto Mary's porch. Sheldon moved with the bowl for his feedings but never ate on the porch if we were present. Sheldon's trust issues persisted, but our enticement efforts, at the very least, produced the desired effect of drawing him closer to us and the house we hoped he'd move into someday. Mary and I couldn't begin to know how much love and patience it would take for Sheldon to finally decide.

Fears and Tears

Sheldon was forever look-
ing up. In his wanderings
in the wilderness, an occasional hawk or owl prob-
ably made a swoop in his
direction. Moreover, northern Michigan thunderstorms produce pouring rain, high winds, swaying
trees, lightning strikes, and booming thunder, all
of which must have made him feel like the gates of
hell were yawning open. Even a light rain caused
Sheldon to pace and glance heavenward. His upward
gaze also inspired me to believe he might be looking
to God, to the Universe, for divine protection.

One afternoon I thought Sheldon's fear might
allow me to get him inside. I was sitting out by the
river with Mary and my girlfriend, Shaun, when
we began to hear thunder rumbling in the distance.
Sheldon appeared behind me, and Shaun saw him
immediately. "Tricia! Look behind you! Whose dog
is that?"

I turned around. "Oh, that's Sheldon."

"Sheldon? Who is Sheldon?"

I told Shaun the nutshell version of his story. Meanwhile, Sheldon continued to come closer. "He's never gotten this close to a group before," I said, "especially without a pork steak involved." The distant thunder sounded again, reminding me of his terror. "Oh God, he's terrified of thunderstorms and he hears the one that's coming."

Sheldon desperately wanted to come to us, to seek comfort and shelter from the oncoming storm. We attempted to coax him closer, speaking to him in our most calm and soothing voices. I propped the sunroom door open and encouraged him to come inside. He walked up to the door, looked inside at me, then checked the lawn behind him and, of course, the sky above.

It almost worked, but the storm was moving in fast and Sheldon had decisions to make. In my opinion, he chose incorrectly. He fled.

Shaun, Mary, and I stood dejected and defeated, staring at each other. Finally, Shaun spoke. "Tricia, I've rescued many abused dogs who are easily scared as a result of their mistreatment. That dog is terrified and has obviously been abused. If you ever find out who his owners are, don't contact them. They don't deserve to get him back."

Those words made an impression.

Weeks after we attempted to lure Sheldon inside, another storm moved in. It was a doozy, waking both Mary and me in our separate quarters. We didn't need to be near Sheldon to know he was terrified, a knowledge that caused us great anguish and, as on so many previous occasions, a sleepless night. The next day we both admitted to lying in bed crying, worried sick about Sheldon. We hoped in vain he had hunkered down in his hut during the storm, but we knew better. He always ran, exposing himself to the elements that so terrorized him.

"Have you seen Sheldon since the storm?" Mary asked a few days later.

"No," I said, "have you?"

A simple "No" was her sad reply.

We watched for him at Rivershire and kept an eye out on River Road as we came and went, but there were no Sheldon sightings. We started losing hope, spirits falling, fearing the worst. Out in the woods he was susceptible to attack by all kinds of wildlife, including coyote, bear, and birds of prey. Our hearts ached.

Weeks passed, and I began to comprehend how deeply I cared about this dog I had never even touched. A new appreciation for love and its possibilities began growing inside me. Every day I sent good energy out to the Universe, intent on Sheldon's well-being and safe return.

Fear not, for the Rivershire magnet is strong.

As I left for work one morning, I looked, as I always did, toward Sheldon's house. And there he stood, looking at me like nothing had happened. I stopped, put down the passenger side window and asked, "Where have you been? We've been worried sick!" He gazed at me with those gorgeous eyes, one brown and one blue, then laid down in the scrub.

One day, while Mary sat on her small porch

reading, Sheldon joined her there, walking closely past her—an unprecedented encounter without the enticement of food or rumble of thunder. Noticing his bicolored eyes up closely, Mary thought one looked cloudy and wondered if perhaps he was partially blind, failing to see her sitting there as a result. However, no other behavior beyond that moment of courage suggested blindness. He simply turned a metaphorical blind eye to his fear and let trust prevail temporarily. Or, he thought Mary had turned to stone.

We tucked these signs of encouragement away in a reserve of hope to draw upon when Sheldon retreated, trusting that someday he would believe in us as much as we believed in him. Our lives carried on in this manner and, for the time being, it was enough.

Moving On

Several months before Mary moved to northern Michigan, she and her friend, Maggie, joined a group from northwestern Ohio on a trip to Hawaii. They quickly got acquainted with a man in their group named Jim, along with his travel companion. The four became friends and had a great time together in Hawaii. At some point, Jim received the nickname Spanky; I never did find out why, and I am pretty sure I don't want to know.

When Mary moved north, she and Jim stayed in touch. On several occasions, when he came up to help a friend remodel a cottage on a nearby lake, Jim called Mary and took her out to dinner. Friendship evolved into something more, and Mary began traveling to Ohio to visit her Spanky. One day, Jim invited her to move into his home in Bowling Green, Ohio. Mary accepted.

Sheldon, the cats, and I were about to have Rivershire to ourselves, except for those times when Sandra came north to visit. It would have been a nice send-off had Sheldon decided to move inside before Mary moved on, but it was not meant to be.

On September 21, 2007, Mary finished loading her car for the trek to Bowling Green. Before following the moving truck carrying the rest of her possessions out of the driveway, Mary took one last look toward the pole barn. Sure enough, there was Sheldon lying in the scrub, watching. "Hey Sheldon. I'm going to Ohio to live with Spanky," Mary said. "You be a good boy. Don't run off. You stay right here where you belong. I'm going to miss you, but I'll come visit. And eat your peas, they're good for you." With that, Mary and I hugged good-bye before she climbed into her car and headed south.

First Touch

By the spring of 2008, Mary had been happily residing in Ohio for over six months. Sheldon made it through his second winter since we first provided him with food and the shelter of the Shit-Shed. As was his pattern, he disappeared at times, but just when I thought I might never see him again he always returned to Rivershire.

That summer my cousin Ann, who lived in New Jersey, visited Rivershire for the second time. She was helping her siblings facilitate her mom's move to Indiana from our hometown in Ohio, and, when she required a reprieve, drove the four-and-a-half hours north for a much-needed dose of sanctuary and solitude. Becki and I often made the same trek in reverse during this time, because our mother was in failing health. Often when we were in our hometown to visit our mom, Ann was there with hers, too. These became special times of connectedness during difficult circumstances, both in Ohio and in northern Michigan.

Sheldon started getting braver during this same period, coming closer to me than ever before. More than two years had passed since I first saw him out my window, yet I still had not touched him. He was incredibly woolly, with three shelves of matted fur across his chest; it pained me to think how uncomfortable this must be for him, the tangled mats pinching and pulling at his skin. His heavy coat— that helped him survive at least two cold winters— was a lot to bear in the heat of summer. I desperately wanted to cut off that matted fur, trim his coat, and give him a bath, but this was impossible to achieve without contact.

One beautiful afternoon during Ann's visit, she and I stepped outside to enjoy some time by the river. Sheldon was hanging around near the apartment and didn't retreat to the scrub even with the two of us standing nearby. Not only did he not retreat, but he stayed close, coming right beside me with Ann only a few feet away. I talked to him for several minutes, and he continued to hang by my side. I decided to make my move.

I reached down, slowly and carefully, still talking to him. My fingers touched his sweet head. He still didn't move. I slowly and tentatively stroked his head. "Ann, don't move. You're witnessing a miracle. This is the first time I have ever been able to touch him. I'm so glad you're here to see, because there are a few people who would never believe it." I kept petting Sheldon while I slid my hand down the back of his head to his neck. It would be a major accomplishment if I could remove his collar during this monumental moment of physical interaction. I moved slowly, carefully, speaking to Sheldon while he continued to let me pet him. My fingers touched the collar and I rotated it around his neck, finding the clasp, which I ever so gently squeezed. As I felt the collar loosen I gave it a soft-but-swift tug. I stood up with the collar in my hand as a surprised and startled Sheldon took off for the scrub.

The red collar hung from my hand. No tags. No clues. No answers. That knowledge, although important, was dwarfed by a lingering sensation of tingling on the tips of my fingers. I knew what it felt like to touch Sheldon. More importantly, he knew what it felt like to be touched again in a loving, caring way. I was quaking with excitement and joy. The lack of identifying tags was actually a relief: had they existed, I would have felt a sense of responsibility to make contact with the humans who put the collar on Sheldon. I could still hear Shaun saying, "That dog is terrified and has obviously been abused. If you ever find out who his owners are, don't contact them. They don't deserve to get him back." With no more information than I had previously, I didn't have to make that decision.

The message of that tag-free collar was immediately clear to me. Sheldon and I were right where we belonged, brought together by universal forces at a place called Rivershire. It was a moment laced with fresh hope. Maybe I *could* get him to trust me. Maybe I *could* get him into the house someday! What once felt so daunting suddenly seemed possible. With every passing day, every word, every pork steak, and at last a simple touch, Sheldon and I had become more deeply connected. I was beaming with love and joy.

That touch created a magic spark between us. Over the next several weeks Sheldon and I continued to have moments of physical connection. I sat on the uninhabited apartment's stoop and talked to him, calling him to me. He ventured near on several occasions, allowing me to pet him for a bit. He even let me cut away at those terrible clumps of matted fur on his chest. I was amazed he let me bring scissors near him, considering that, up until very recently, he wouldn't even allow me to touch him. I carefully chopped away at the clumps of matted fur without getting too close to his skin.

This was great progress, completely on Sheldon's terms. He took the brave step of trusting me with a sharp instrument as trade-off for great relief. He tolerated the procedure for only as long as suited him. After a few chunks were removed he retreated to the safety zone near his house, watching me from there. Enough for one day. Our grooming sessions continued but only when Sheldon was in the mood. It was a delicate dance.

One might wonder: If Sheldon allowed me to pet him and cut off chucks of matted fur, why couldn't I just pick him up and carry him inside? The answer is simple. Sheldon wasn't ready. He was still very skittish, and any sudden movements sent him scampering. One day, not long after I touched him for the first time, I did pick him up. When he realized his feet weren't touching the ground, his little legs began running a mile a minute in mid-air, like a crazed wind-up toy squirming in my hands. I set him down before he had a chance to wrench himself free and fall. Legs already pumping, he ran for the safety of his hut the second his paws hit the ground. We had just begun to physically connect and, like all things Sheldon, baby steps, my friends, baby steps.

Mom's Farewell

The summer of 2008 ended up being full of significant occurrences. Sandra and I decided to partner in a second endeavor, that of owning and operating a small retail space at the Village of Grand Traverse Commons, a redevelopment project of the former State Hospital grounds in Traverse City. Sandra owned the operation, and I eventually served as the manager. The process of preparing for opening day had been ongoing for months. Once open, the store would feature an array of delectable food items, including ice cream and gelato, sweet treats and snacks.

While getting ready for opening day was significant, what was going on with our mom would prove far more memorable—which is ironic, because Mom had dementia. Mom's memory had been waning for several years, eventually reaching a point where even the names of her children were lost to her.

Our dad passed away in 2001; after his death, we watched Mom decline. Initially she did all right, but we began noticing signs of memory loss and odd behavior, forcing us kids to the conclusion that she couldn't safely reside in her home anymore. There is a nice retirement facility in our hometown, and we were able to get Mom a room in the assisted-living wing.

While this was better than having her live alone, it was not a good fit for her. She quickly became more confused, incapable of operating the television or the microwave. For me, the most torturous part of her dementia came at the end of each visit, with Mom clinging to us as we left, begging us to take her wherever we were going. This was, of course, impossible, but try explaining that to her. Each visit ended in agonizing and heart-breaking tearful goodbyes, Mom looking out the window as we walked away. On other occasions she followed us out, declaring that she was going along. A resident or staff member of the facility would take her by the arm and lead our crying mother back inside. Few moments in my life have caused me heartache like I felt during those inevitable farewells.

It became clear to my family (and the staff of the care facility) that the assisted-living wing wasn't working for Mom. Her name was placed on the waiting list for an available room in the Alzheimer's/Dementia wing. Fortunately, one blessed day, a room opened up. That's the sad truth about homes housing the elderly and ill: One family's loss—even though it may be a day of blessed relief for everyone—is another family's opportunity. On the day Mom got her new room, it was like the sky opened up and rays of sunlight shone down on her world. Mom adjusted well to her new living quarters. She relaxed and ceased clinging and crying when we left. She seemed at peace. Being attended to by specialized professionals and receiving medical care, physical attention, and emotional interaction relative to her condition, Mom settled in and contentedly continued her journey in what appeared to be peaceful oblivion. Even when she reached the point where she no longer knew the names of her nine kids, she still lit up with a sparkle in her eyes when we came into the room. When I asked her, as I did each visit—"Mom, who am I?"— she smiled, chuckled, and said, "I don't know," in a sweet, singsong-y voice that conveyed, "and it's okay that I don't know, but I'm pretty sure I love you, whoever you are." That was enough for me.

What didn't fade from Mom's memory were hymns, the music of her life. It was a beautiful and amazing thing to behold—when someone played hymns on the piano, Mom sang along without aid of the hymnal. The words and notes were all there, deeply embedded in Mom's head and heart where they had been all her life. They did not fail her when she needed them the most.

In the spring of 2008, Mom fell and broke her hip. Sandra asked me, "Do you think it's the beginning of the end?" Indeed I did. We all did.

Weeks passed. Trips were made to Ohio, and eventually Becki and I got the call that we should

come home, as Mom was expected to pass soon. I
was long past the point where I became ready for
her to die. I prayed for it. As we sat by her bed for
the last time, Sandra, Becki, and I lovingly pleaded
with her to let go, to leave, to go be with Dad. Mom
was completely comatose by this point. I held a
stuffed bear of hers while Handel's *Messiah* played
on her CD player. Mom loved Handel's *Messiah*. I
clutched the bear close because it did a great job of
catching my tears.

Mom wasn't quite ready to let go, so Becki and I
headed north once again to wait for the call. This
came in the early hours of July 19, just after 1:00
a.m. Becki rang me to say she had been contacted
by our oldest sister Suz, who (along with my broth-
ers, Bob and Butch, and their wives, Joyce and
Sharon) had stood by Mom's bed, singing hymns
and holding her hands as she finally let go and left
this world.

After her call I lay awake for some time, very
much at peace. A few tears rolled as I focused on
being aware of any presence I might sense as Mom's
spirit moved on. I experienced nothing earth-shat-
tering but was simply present and in tune during
that significant moment of transition.

Mom was often called a saint, although she
would never use that as a description of herself.
She was too humble for that. My ex-husband called
her Mother Teresa because of her caring, nonjudg-
mental nature. I don't have a lot of experience with
saints, so it's hard to make a comparison, but if
Mom was one then she was an open-minded saint,

which would seem to me to be an important saintly quality.

Mom loved her life, her family, and her God. She was compassionate and kind; I never heard her say a truly negative thing about anyone. I felt very close to her and learned so much from her. She amazed me in many ways.

I always thought the greatest heartbreak of my life would be the day Mom died. Instead, after experiencing Mom in the throes of dementia, witnessing the decline of her physical health and the pain she suffered after her fall, I desperately wished for her release more than anything. My mother believed in heaven, and if anyone I have ever met deserved entry, it was Mom.

Still, that didn't make her funeral easy. Knowing I would never again kiss her soft cheek, hear her sweet giggle, or see her eyes light up upon my entrance caused me great heartache. I will forever miss her gentle spirit. Memories will have to serve.

Upon my return to Michigan after her funeral in Ohio, I found Sheldon waiting by the driveway. I said my goodbyes to Becki and Ronnie (they had dropped me off at Rivershire), poured myself a glass of wine, and headed outside to talk with him.

"Sheldon, the funeral was beautiful. Just like her. It was the kind of service she would have wanted, sweet and simple. It fit her so well. Hymns, scripture, and a few words about her goodness, her kindness, her generosity—although that would have embarrassed her. Almost everyone I spoke with said over and over how they never heard her speak ill of anyone. That's a noble quality. She was a special person; you would have loved her and she would have loved you. I wish she could have met you, but she's been too far gone mentally to travel north in recent years. She never was able to visit Rivershire. That's a tragedy. I wish she could have come here at least once."

Sheldon did what he did best. He listened. He stayed close, never interrupting, just listening. I told him, "Sheldon, it's time to come inside, don't you think? It's going to be winter soon enough, and I simply can't bear to think of you living outside again this year. I want you to really think about it." I then looked upward, like Sheldon did so often, and said, "Mom, help me with this one. From one sweet spirit to another, let Sheldon know that it will be okay. Meanwhile, I'll start convincing the cats."

Storm-Weather Friends and Boiling-Point Gods

Thunderstorms continued to haunt Sheldon. With Mary gone, I alone was left to fret about Sheldon and feel the heartbreak of his terror. Two incidents in particular stick out in my memory.

With his heightened canine senses Sheldon perceived storms well before I did, either through the sound of distant thunder or a change in atmospheric pressure. One Sunday afternoon a storm began moving across northern Michigan, causing Sheldon to pace around the property. I went outside to try my luck at coaxing him inside. Afraid of the outdoor elements, and trusting me more day by day, it stood to reason that Sheldon would seek shelter inside a sturdy structure, away from the wind and approaching wicked weather. My reasoning and Sheldon's leaned in opposite directions.

The sky turned dark and the thunder rolled as I stood holding open the door for Sheldon. He looked at me, then at the door. Then, he turned and began running.

I followed as he ran up the driveway and out onto River Road. I held my breath, terrified he would be hit by a car on our busy road. He continued running down the middle of the street as I called out to him, trying to keep my voice calm and encouraging even though I was in a state of distress. "Sheldon! Come here boy! Sheldon! Sheldon! Come on, buddy!" I stood in the road, risking life and limb, just like Sheldon. There was, once again, nothing I could do to stop or protect him. He was faster than me; all I could do was watch and pray he got off the road before a car came. Devastation and heartbreak struck me anew. This time, however, it hurt more than ever before. Why, for the love of God, would he not come into a safe place with someone he was beginning to trust? What had happened to this poor, sweet dog that would cause him to run down a dangerous road into an impending storm instead of coming inside to be protected and loved? Many questions; absolutely no answers.

I was so damn sad. I hurt all over. I went inside and lay down on my bed. I didn't care that it was the middle of the afternoon or if I stayed in bed the rest of the day. Tears wet my cheeks. I was emotionally spent and didn't know when I had ever felt so lonely.

Then, I heard the voices. "Tricia! Tricia!" At first I thought I was hearing things, losing my mind, or both. But the voices persisted. "Tricia! Are you home? Tricia!" I went out onto my porch to discover a group of friends pulling kayaks and canoes from the river just as the rain started to fall. With thunder rumbling and lightning visible, I called to the group, "Hurry! Come in! Hurry!" People began pouring into my kitchen for what became an impromptu party that I needed more than any of them could possibly know.

They brought in small coolers and dry bags from which they pulled out beer, wine, and snacks that had been packed for the group float. I reached into my own refrigerator and bar, pulling out any offerings I had to share. For the next hour or so we laughed, talked, drank, and ate while the storm passed overhead. After a time the sky cleared. My friends piled back into their canoes and kayaks, taking off down the river to finish their excursion.

As I went inside after sending these friends on their way, I marveled at what had been given to me that day, both in the form of despair and comfort. Also, I wondered where Sheldon might be and how he had fared in the storm. As usual, it took a week or two for him to return; then there he was, sitting next to his hut as I left for work as though nothing had happened.

The second memorable storm occurred one day as I was heading into town to go to work. It had just started raining—pouring, actually. I didn't see Sheldon as I left my driveway and hoped that by some miracle he might actually have taken shelter from the storm inside his house, although I worried the metal Shit-Shed would be struck by lightning. As I drove up River Road, I saw something sitting by my neighbor's mailbox. I approached slowly, recognizing it was an animal that could dart into the road at any moment. As I passed I comprehended it was not just any animal, but *Sheldon*, lying there, gazing at the road watching traffic go by in the pouring rain.

My spirit sank. My stomach clenched. I was overwhelmed with a combination of devastation and rage. My heart broke while my anger soared. I felt my hopes and dreams for the life I imagined Sheldon and I sharing together splinter, each shard stabbing into my heart and soul. I took a page from Sheldon's life story and looked up, but I didn't send a prayer for help or consolation. Instead I let go with a profanity-laced rant, spewing my grief, anger, and frustration over a situation I had poured every ounce of myself into, only to watch this lost and wayward Sheltie sit alongside a busy road getting soaked to the core in the cold rain.

I felt helpless and mad and sad and lost. There was nothing I could do, except yell at the god-of-stray-dogs-who-are-too-damn-stubborn-to-come-in-the-house-that-is-offered-to-them. I had reached a breaking point, at least for the moment.

Perhaps using such a tone when talking to God or the Universe is ill-advised, but I was angry. I had thrown Sheldon many a bone, typically of the pork steak variety, and now I needed someone to throw one my way. I couldn't endure the heartbreak of loving a dog that insisted on braving the elements while I fretted and worried endlessly about his well-being. I was done. Either he was going to come in, or I was going to let go, at least to the extent where I accepted I had an outdoor dog who lived in a Shit-Shed and ate whatever I threw his way, but would never grant me the pleasure and relief of living inside my home.

Apparently, something in my tirade worked. The boiling point of my frustration must have reached that particular god who had Sheldon on its agenda, because something was about to give. Actually, someone was about to give in.

We're Coming In

A week or so after I spotted a soaking-wet Sheldon lying next to the neighbor's mailbox, he resurfaced at Rivershire. He took up his usual position next to his hut, waiting patiently for the next pork steak. I, of course, obliged. My anger and frustration had subsided; I was never actually mad at Sheldon, of course, but rather mad at the situation, at the roller coaster ride that was our relationship. I fully accepted the fact that, even though I would keep enticing him to come inside, it was entirely his call. He needed to be ready to move in.

I heard the *Farmers' Almanac* predicted a severe winter ahead. The two previous winters at Rivershire had been relatively mild by northern Michigan standards. As difficult as it had been for him to endure the conditions of the past two years, it was about to get brutal for Sheldon if the predictions of sub-zero days played out in the coming months. Furthermore, I was concerned that if we got the amount of snow predicted, Sheldon might not be able to get in or out of his house during such a weather event. I foresaw a great deal of snow shoveling in my future and would be happy to do it, but I fretted about how he would fare in severe snowstorms. I needed to explain all of this to him over a nice pork steak dinner.

The pork steak sizzled on the grill. Sheldon approached and assumed his usual position—lying down, paws slightly in front of him, head up, ears perked, nose in the air—taking in the scents and sounds he associated with the tastiest of morsels. His eyes, naturally, searched the sky lest some crazed hawk decided either he or the pork steak were to be claimed and carried off.

"Okay buddy, here's the drill. This winter is going to be rough. I can't bear to watch you live out in the elements any more. It will not be easy for you. Can you understand that? I will never hurt you, Sheldon. Oh, I'm sure I'll make mistakes. Do you know that I've never had an indoor dog? Yep, only cats. My intentions are good, and I'll do my best to take care of you. Please, please come in. Please."

When the pork steak was done, cooked medium rare as we both liked it, I removed it from the fire and turned off the grill. As always I cut around the bone, leaving some nice tidbits of pork attached, and placed it on a platter to cool before giving it to Sheldon. My portion went back on the grill to stay warm.

When Sheldon's bone was cool enough I took it

in my hand, squatted down arm outstretched, and watched my little guy timidly approach. He took the bone tenderly from between my fingers and trotted off to his safe zone, where he feasted upon the greatest treat of all—well, next to a warm bed and temperature-controlled environment, anyway. If only Sheldon would see it that way.

"Please give it some serious thought," I called over to him. "It's already October. Winter may come on fast and furious this year. Let's get you moved in soon so we have some time to adapt before the shit hits the fan. Deal?"

Sheldon's blue eye and brown eye gazed at me while he chomped, pork bone sticking out of the side of his mouth. I got the sense he might at least consider it. I went inside and enjoyed my dinner, too.

Earlier in the year, I'd begun a relationship with someone I met the previous October at my annual Halloween party. Now, nearly a year later, right about the time of my conversation with Sheldon over pork steak, a new tenant moved into the apartment at Rivershire. The relationship guy and the new tenant were one and the same. I'll call him Ted.

After Ted moved in, he occasionally propped the front door of the apartment open on nice days to encourage Sheldon to walk in. Sheldon ventured close at times, and (once!) he did step inside, but became so freaked out when the door closed behind him that he darted frantically around the living room in an effort to escape. Concerned for his well-being, Ted opened the door and let him back out. While greatly disappointed in the outcome of that experiment, I also had some renewed hope that Sheldon was considering my offer to come inside.

Saturday, October 11, 2008, began without fanfare. No blaring trumpets appeared in the sky, heralding the arrival of one of the most significant days of my life. I don't recall what was on my agenda that afternoon, but I had to be somewhere. Whatever took me from the river that day didn't last long, and I returned by late afternoon, home in time to make dinner and relax by the river on what was a lovely fall day. I had no plans other than to eat and watch college football. Seemed like a perfect Saturday evening to me. Little did I know, Sheldon had other plans.

When I got home Sheldon was hanging out in front of the apartment, pacing and staying close. "What's going on, buddy?" I asked. I loved those wonderful moments when Sheldon didn't run off as I approached. I bent down and was permitted the privilege of petting him. He had allowed me to do this often enough that the three shelves of matted and burr-laden fur on his chest were trimmed down considerably. "Tell you what. We'll open that door, and why don't you walk right on in? Just don't freak out this time."

I had decided the best way to get Sheldon inside would be by using the apartment as a portal. My front door was on a raised porch which Sheldon never ventured up onto, not even once to the best of my knowledge. Mary and I had fed Sheldon on the apartment porch—which was at ground level, with no steps at all—so he was accustomed to being there.

My other thought process associated with starting Sheldon off in the apartment had to do with Snickers and Gracie. Gracie had never been around dogs, and I feared abruptly adding another animal, especially a dog, might ratchet up the crazy in her. Snickers acquired canine experience during a time when she and I resided in an apartment that shared space with a neighbor and his dog. Snickers wanted nothing to do with that dog, except to hiss at him whenever he ventured near, and I assumed she would behave the same way with Sheldon. I reasoned that if I could gradually introduce all three, things might go more smoothly. But first, Sheldon would have to walk through the portal into a new, strange world.

Ted opened the apartment's front door as I stood nearby. "There you go! Go on! Go on in," I said, in my most chipper of voices. Instead, Sheldon wandered back toward his hut. "Oh Sheldon. You know what, forget it. I'm going to change my clothes, make dinner, watch football, relax. Let me know if you change your mind."

I returned in more comfortable attire with the intention of starting the grill. What happened instead lives in Rivershire legend as a truly miraculous moment. Sheldon walked up to me and stood by my side. I looked at Ted, who had closed his door by now. "I'm going to pick him up and see what happens," I said. I had done it once before with less than positive results, but, what the hell, it was time to try again. Maybe Sheldon needed the welcoming affirmation of being carried inside. Sometimes, we all need a little help letting go of our fears, insecurities, and heavy burdens. There have been times in my life when I wished someone would pick me up and carry me in the right direction; in a way, I felt I had been picked up and carried to Rivershire. Maybe Sheldon needed the same mode of transportation.

I bent down and picked him up in the same manner as before, around his middle—which allowed all four legs to hang straight down. I expected to see his little legs start peddling, but to my complete delight he did nothing of the sort. Actually, he did nothing at all. He didn't move a muscle. Sheldon was as ready to go inside as he was ever going to be.

I looked at Ted and spoke the words I had been wanting to say for a long, long time. "Open the door, we're coming in." Together, Sheldon and I walked through the portal.

The miracles continued. Sheldon didn't race around the apartment seeking an exit when I first set him down. Ted and I spread towels on the floor, and I carefully began cutting fur off of Sheldon. He barely moved. He simply stood there, accepting what was happening to him. When the initial trim was complete, I carried him upstairs and ran water into the tub. I expected a battle upon putting him in the few inches of water, but I didn't get one. He just stood there, stock-still, and let us give him a bath. He was done living on the lam, ready to trade the lam for the lap of luxury—well, luxury as far as he was concerned. This place beat the hell out of the Shit-Shed.

For three hours we were consumed with cutting and bathing. Fresh, clean water was repeatedly transformed into mud baths. And Sheldon smelled. Oh my, did he smell! He had poop stuck to his backside, matted in his fur. That moment of discovery caused some gagging on my part.

The tub was filled and drained at least three or four times. With every bath, Sheldon stood still and allowed it to happen. At one point I realized I had tears in my eyes, with a few running down my face. I couldn't believe this was happening—I was overwhelmed with joy. And while my cheeks were wet with tears, the rest of me was completely and thoroughly soaked with dirty bath water. I, too, was going to need a bath when the ordeal was through.

Sheldon's resignation and patience with the bathing process also held fast where fur-cutting was concerned. As I cut off chuck after chunk of matted fur, he stood still and accepted the grooming without any nipping, growling, or fidgeting. I wiped down his body, feeling it becoming smaller after every cutting. I was extra-careful as I cut, making sure to never nip his skin. The pile of matted fur on the floor filled a brown paper grocery sack. I could only imagine how good it felt for Sheldon to get the stench, filth, and fur off his small, sweet body. I knew he wasn't a large dog, but with at least two-and-a-half years of fur growth removed, he resembled a tiny little lamb.

"There's no going back now, buddy. You can't survive outside without all that fur. You just became an indoor doggie."

And so it began. What lie ahead for both of us couldn't be known at the time, but the next phase of our journey as comrades began that day. October 11 will always be Happy Sheldon Day for me.

Is There
a Psychiatrist
in the House?

I awoke the next morning
to the dawning realiza-
tion that Sheldon was inside the house. A pile of
blankets in the apartment was his bed that first
night. I hoped he felt safe.

I was afraid Sheldon would retreat to the woods
upon being let out to relieve himself. Initially I
took him out on a leash, which he accepted well,
but I could tell he wanted to do a little sniffing and
wandering in order to do his business. I had an
Invisible Fence system installed, only to discover
this was a total waste of money. While Sheldon,
clearly a very intelligent animal, easily grasped
the training involved, he simply didn't need the
non-evident fence. Sheldon would barely leave the
porch.

His pattern was to wander into the yard to relieve
himself, then immediately retreat to the apartment's back porch. It was clear he now accepted

that a soft bed and temperature-controlled environment were enjoyable luxuries. He had decided one thing for sure; he was going nowhere.

I soon discovered that getting Sheldon to eat would take an act of Congress. The days of pork steak and wedding food were over. Sheldon needed a healthy dog diet and regular feeding regimen.

His ability to eat was based on emotion. He was timid, afraid, and unsure, always desperate to please. There were schedules and expectations. Sheldon was trying to figure out who was in charge—me, Ted, or both. He wanted to please both of us, but didn't know how, especially considering Ted and I had two very different approaches to canine care. All of that affected his appetite. To encourage him, I placed a bowl containing a combination of kibble mixed with canned food into his bed, crawling in alongside Sheldon. His bed, an official one purchased at a pet store, was his new safe zone, located by the kitchen table in the apartment. I went over there daily to feed Sheldon, cheering him on with my mantra: "Here you go, Sheldon! Eat your meat! Good boy."

And so our feeding ritual began. I squeezed myself into the bed next to Sheldon, my legs outstretched on the floor with his bowl tucked between us. After I encouraged him to eat I turned my gaze away, attempting an air of aloofness that conveyed "no one is watching you eat. I am completely ignoring you but here for comfort and encouragement." I took a book and my phone to his bed with me,

since I was often there for as long as twenty minutes while Sheldon decided if eating his meat was
something he was interested in doing. More often
than not I finally rose from Sheldon's bed with my
ass completely asleep, pins and needles prickling
my legs. I took his bowl and its slightly eaten remnants to store in the refrigerator until our next
attempt at dining.

Yes, I was crazy. Or at least crazy about Sheldon.
I had no indoor dog experience on my pet resume,
let alone any experience with one who wouldn't eat.
I was at a loss. Every dog I ever observed in friends'
and family members' homes devoured their meals.
Not Sheldon.

To further complicate matters, something
wasn't sitting well in Sheldon's stomach. We
repeatedly came home to find ugly accidents on the
floor—along with a very embarrassed puppy. His
upset tummy was most likely responsible for his
less than voracious appetite; for all I knew, he had
diarrhea episodes while living outside. I attempted
to adjust his diet so that he would be healthy, not
just digestively speaking, but mentally and emotionally as well. How could I ever go away on vacation, leaving his care to someone else, if Sheldon
couldn't approach a meal without having a licensed
psychiatrist and nutritionist on the premises?
Simply from the perspective of daily life, my morn-
ings and evenings revolved around getting him to
eat and then go potty so I could get on with my day.
I still had to work, after all.

One day I took Sheldon over to my side of the

house to begin introducing him to Snickers and Gracie. There was some moist cat food left on the girls' plates on the floor. Sheldon swooped in and cleaned both plates promptly. Okay, new approach.

It was important for Sheldon to like what I fed him, but it also had to be healthy and not disrupt his sensitive system. Apparently all aspects of Sheldon, both in character and internal workings, were of a sensitive nature. The veterinarian was a great help in this area, as was a pill for treating intestinal flare-ups. After some trial and error, we discovered a veterinarian-prescribed food that Sheldon enjoyed and was good for his tender system. The cat's canned food didn't appear to be upsetting his tummy, so I mixed in a bit of that for added enticement.

Eventually I figured it out, although feeding Sheldon was always a bit of a song and dance routine. I was both singer and dancer. Sheldon was the fiddler.

A routine developed that went like this. Both in the morning and evening, I went to the apartment and mixed some dry food with a little cat food while I talked to Sheldon, conjuring all the exuberance I could muster. "Would you like something to eat? Would Sheldon like to eat his meat? Of course he would! Of course he would! Who wouldn't want to eat their meat!" Then I'd crawl in his bed with him and put the bowl down. Some of my happiest moments of our early days together were those times when Sheldon ate his food while I sat at his side, followed by him heading to the door to go out and do his business. Often, I was elated nearly to the point of tears.

Not only was eating an issue for Sheldon, but riding in the car was a study in neurosis of textbook proportions. Look up the word "neurosis" in the dictionary, and there you will find a photo of Sheldon and me in a 2007 Subaru Impreza wagon. (There may also be a photo of us sitting in his doggie bed with his food bowl between us. And yes, it's not lost on me that I, too, am in the photo. Know thyself.)

Sheldon jumped into the car with only a little bit of encouragement, but once we started moving he became highly agitated, his skittish, nervous nature cranking into overdrive. There was a great deal of panting and pacing involved, as well as mad leaping from the front seat to the back. I would have been concerned about him wracking his testicles on the center console, but these had been expertly removed by the veterinarian soon after his move inside. He also tried to climb on my lap. I did not allow this distractingly dangerous behavior. Sheldon was repeatedly denied access, and he soon learned it was front seat or back seat, but not my seat.

I was concerned about Sheldon. I wanted him to be a happy and healthy dog, both physically and emotionally. I knew he had been through a lot, but the specifics were vague. Many questions, no answers. Nearly three years had passed since I spotted him for the first time. He was my dog, and it was my responsibility to take good care of him. I took that responsibility very seriously.

I discussed all issues with my veterinarian, and it was suggested that perhaps doggie training, including socialization techniques with a qualified professional, might help. I figured it sure couldn't hurt. A local, well-respected trainer was recommended, so I gave him a call and booked us into his next round of sessions. The trainer's name was Sam, and he was able to share a good deal of information about Shelties in general, offering me reassurance over the phone. I felt better after speaking with Sam, and soon thereafter Sheldon and I went to our first group dog training session, mostly to try and acclimate him to being around other dogs.

Upon arriving at doggie school, already upset at having been taken on a car ride, Sheldon pulled on his leash, heading toward the door we had just entered. He was done before we even got started! I, attempting to be the one in charge, tugged him away from the door, determined to give training a chance.

During these sessions I discovered not only how smart Sheldon was but that he had apparently been trained in his previous mystery life. His intense desire to leave class prompted him to quickly absorb and respond to the commands and techniques. Once completed he'd head for the exit, as though to say, "There! That's done. Let's go."

Sheldon wasn't the only one who needed training, which was already obvious to me and anyone who witnessed our mealtime antics. I was hoping class would help me understand dogs—mostly my dog—and how they functioned. I learned how to give commands, including what to say and the tone of voice in which to say it. I was shown how to reward good behavior and correct improper behavior. However, training Sheldon didn't work the same way as it did for other dogs in the class. He was too nervous in the foreign and stimulating environment to accept pocket treats as a reward for performing tasks. Sheldon was a finicky eater in his own home. Consuming anything, even the tastiest of treats like freeze-dried beef liver, the caviar of treats in Sheldon's opinion, was the last thing on his mind when surrounded by a horde of seemingly insane dogs who were jumping, barking, and pulling on their leashes like crazed lunatics. It was clear to Sheldon that they needed training; he, in his own estimation, did not. He just needed to get the hell out of there, even though that meant getting back in the damn car. If that's what it took to get home and settled into his comfort zone, so be it. Forget the treats: going home was the ultimate reward.

After a time, we stopped going to doggie school. The reasons were twofold. One involved Sheldon's diarrhea attacks, which I was attempting to get under control. Anxiety appeared to trigger episodes, and the stress Sheldon experienced during training sessions exacerbated this situation. It took trial and error, plus a supply of tablets on hand at all times, to get Sheldon's stomach issues regulated. The second reason we stopped attending class was that I planned on going to Florida for two weeks, so at the very least we would miss two sessions.

I hated to leave Sheldon, but the Florida trip was something of a necessity. A financial necessity. I was going, as I had many years prior, to work at a large heavy equipment auction in Kissimmee for a company previously owned by my family.

Little did I know my trip to Florida would be a step in the right direction for Sheldon.

Sleepover Therapy

I had important decisions to make involving where Sheldon would stay while I was gone. I knew Snickers and Gracie could adapt to any sitter, but didn't know how Sheldon would fare. He was still living in the apartment, and I wasn't going to leave him there with Ted, who had no tolerance for the feeding routine. I was afraid Sheldon would starve.

Abruptly moving Sheldon in with the cats was not an option. I needed to be the one to orchestrate that change and be home for the adjustment period. Expecting the pet sitter to handle that was a job way above her pay scale. Then, I had an idea.

I called my usual pet sitter, asking if she was available to stay at the house with the cats. Done. Then, I called Becki to see how she and Ronnie felt about keeping Sheldon at their place while I was away. I thought maybe it would do good for Sheldon to stay with people who loved him, along with a fellow canine he had met on a few occasions. Maybe, without me there, Sheldon and his cousin

Bowie (Becki and Ronnie's big, wonderful, lovable, and rather dopey Golden Retriever) would form a bond. Becki and Ronnie agreed to give it a try. None of us knew what might transpire, but we all agreed it would be interesting to find out.

I was sure the greatest challenge facing Becki and Ronnie during Sheldon's two-week-long sleepover would be getting him to eat. A new environment would be enough to throw Sheldon off his routine, without even factoring Bowie into the equation. Bowie took all of thirty seconds to down his meal and would eat absolutely anything within his reach. Once, while visiting Becki and Ronnie, I dropped an open jar of minced garlic on the floor. Thank goodness the jar didn't shatter: Bowie licked up the splattered contents so quickly I had no time to react. I was almost as stunned that a dog would want to eat an entire jar of garlic as I was by the speed at which he ate it! Sheldon would need to eat faster than he did at home or find a way to defend his dinner against a dog four times his size. If not, he might be down to his living-on-the-lam weight by the time I returned.

I took Sheldon and all his supplies—bed, bowls, food, freeze-dried liver treats, tablets for his intestinal distress, harness, leash, and a laundry list of detailed instructions—over to Becki and Ronnie's house before I headed for the airport. Leaving was the hardest part for both of us, probably mostly me. When I got in my car, started it, and looked up, there was Sheldon peering longingly at me through a floor-to-ceiling window next to the front door. My heart broke, and it took everything in my power not to run back into that house, snatch him up, and cancel my trip to Florida. Instead I drove away. About a quarter mile up the road, I pulled over to have a bit of a cry. I told myself to trust that it would be okay. Not only okay, but something we both needed. I was going to miss that dog. I really hoped he didn't miss me. I wanted him to be happy and content in my absence.

What happened next blew our minds. One evening, I called Becki to check in. "You're not going to believe this," she told me. "Last night we threw Bowie's ball down the hall for him to retrieve, like we always do. When he ran after it Sheldon followed, barking frantically, circling Bowie and nipping at his heels. He was herding him. As long as Bowie kept running and retrieving, Sheldon herded him."

"You're kidding me," I said.

"Nope. We couldn't believe our eyes. We almost peed ourselves laughing. Now, they are inseparable. When they're not playing, they lie down by each other. If Sheldon thinks Bowie should be moving faster—or moving at all, for that matter—he starts nipping at his heels. It's just hilarious. The only time they're apart is at night. Bowie sleeps in his bed in our bedroom, and the only place Sheldon wants to sleep is on the ottoman by Ronnie's chair, not his dog bed. He gets on the ottoman when we turn out the lights and stays there all night."

It took getting Sheldon around a retriever for

his natural herding instincts to surface. Shelties are born-and-bred herders. Their full breed name is Shetland Shepherd. I hadn't even thought about this before and had definitely never witnessed Sheldon herd anything. I was amazed. I was thrilled! Sheldon was coming out of his shell.

So it turned out that Bowie—whom no one would accuse of being the smartest dog on the planet—was the psychotherapist we needed all along. This stay-over was a major breakthrough in Sheldon's development, and Cousin Bowie played an integral part. A wonderful doggie friendship developed and evolved during my time away.

As for Sheldon's eating habits, well, this went as we expected. Sheldon didn't become a speedy eater overnight; his finicky approach to dining remained intact. Bowie also remained true to his nature. Realizing that an additional dog in the house meant additional food was being served, Bowie did his best to locate and devour any extra morsels he could find. Becki created a wall of strategically placed chairs laid on their sides around the dining room table to give Sheldon a safe zone underneath, like a doggie feeding corral with a roof. This helped keep Bowie at bay, but Sheldon did his part too, finding the gumption to produce a low growl when Bowie approached the barrier. Bowie found it impossible to navigate the chair legs and crouch low enough to get at Sheldon. In that space, Sheldon's food and treats were his to savor and enjoy at his own pace.

There was a fire inside his belly after all, another

side to the timid, cautious, and skittish little guy that had been through so much. Sheldon was adapting to his new life, his personality accordingly beginning to emerge in many forms.

Upon my return home, Sheldon resumed living in the apartment. This would have been a fine time to move Sheldon into my side of the house; he received a confidence boost from his time spent with Cousin Bowie, resulting in the emergence of a more outgoing personality. Unwisely, I chose to return him to apartment dwelling. There was something about the atmosphere in the apartment that caused Sheldon to revert back to his more timid and unsure nature.

Hindsight being what it is, I believe starting him off in the apartment was an error in judgment. Even though my side of the house contained cats, I was the only person living there. Sheldon and I could have formed our indoor bond without the complications of two people calling the shots. I did what I thought was best at the time, but there were too many conflicting signals for one confused and wayward Sheltie to comprehend.

I recognized there was a problem, so I cranked into high gear my mission to give Sheldon the best life possible. I took him with me whenever I could. On some of our outings we visited Aunt Becki, Uncle Ronnie, and Cousin Bowie. I got to witness first-hand the hilarity of the retrieving and herding. Bowie was a gentle giant, and the two dogs did very well together. When Bowie had enough of his heels being nipped, he let Sheldon know with a low growl and nip of his own in Sheldon's direction. When they weren't playing, they lay on the floor together. They had found a best friend in each other, just what they both needed.

Becoming Enough

The seasons of 2009 mor-
phed one into the next, and
before long summer was
upon us. Summer in northern Michigan is nothing short of spectacular. The natural beauty of the
region—coupled with its moderate, pleasant cli-
mate—makes it a vacation mecca. My family began
vacationing at a camp in Onekama, Michigan, in
the 1940s. Even though I live only an hour away,
I still vacation there. I came north as a child, and
what started as a vacation spot became a part of my
heart and soul. Northern Michigan, with its lakes
great and small, crystal clear streams, lush wood-
lands, and rolling dunes of soft sand, wrapped itself
around me and would not let go. Moving north was
my dream, and one day in 1994 I made it my reality.

My favorite part of the summer remains the
same in adulthood as in childhood. I pack my car
and make the simple trek to Onekama to enjoy some
vacation time in a peaceful town perfectly positioned between Portage Lake and Lake Michigan.
It is the place where my love of northern Michigan

began. I feel a strong need to be there each August for my annual rejuvenation.

The summer of 2009 was no different. I packed my bags, as did Becki and Ronnie, and headed off to Onekama. With the camp's strict no pets policy, Sheldon would not be welcome to join us. He stayed at his favorite vacation spot, Cousin Bowie's house, under the capable care of Vicki, Bowie's regular pet sitter.

I came back from Onekama one week later and picked up Sheldon. Things were going to be different upon our return to Rivershire. Sheldon wasn't going to live in the apartment anymore; he was moving in with me and the cats. Ted was moving on, and Sheldon could move in where he belonged.

Our cohabitation became a whirlwind involving four creatures: myself, Sheldon, Snickers, and Gracie. We got acclimated to living in the same space with each other. Sheldon dealt with this in his usual way—by staying in bed. Although now it was my bed where he preferred to stay. I placed his dog bed at the foot of mine, but why stay there, on the same level as those pesky cats, when one can hang out on the cozy comfort of a king-sized bed loaded with fleece blankets and afghans? Of course, those pesky cats liked the big bed too, and before I knew it all three were piled together with little or no hissing involved—unless, of course, Sheldon decided to sniff one of the cats' butts. This would not be tolerated.

Sheldon seldom wandered off my bed, except to

be let out to go potty or if I was taking him somewhere. I resorted to feeding him there in an effort
to establish a safe zone, where Sheldon recognized
his needs would be met without undue pressure to
meet external expectations. I encouraged him to
follow me around the house, and he did so in order
to obey my directive and please me, but eventually
he would give me a timid, downcast look and scurry
back to bed. I reasoned that, in his new environment, there would be an adjustment period.

Simultaneously, I was experiencing my own
adjustment period.

During the latter part of 2009, the smoldering discontent deep within me—which I'd been
attempting to smother for many years—came up
for air, just what it needed to become a raging
inferno. The cocoon I'd wrapped myself in had
become dry and brittle, going up like a matchstick
soaked in lighter fluid to reveal a self that was raw,
scorched, and wounded. I searched madly for some
healing salve but found none. What burned away
left me exposed and vulnerable, and I had no choice
but to look directly at the blisters and assess the
damage.

For far too long I had been squelching feelings
of doubt and despair. The more I attempted to
push them down the more they floated to the surface, bloated and unruly. These feelings began to
gnaw at me in earnest around 2007. One evening
that summer, I told my friend Barbie that I found
no joy in anything. Two years later, my pain could
no longer be ignored.

I began to assess my agony. Rational thought dictated all was well in my world; I had a special home, good health, great friends, a loving family, and dear pets. Yet, the agony was real and, while all the bounty in my life offered sustenance, there remained a lacking element I needed to define in order to truly survive. So, I dove inside to see what would surface. "You've never been truly loved," said a small voice. "That is what you've always desired." This was not, of course, entirely true. I certainly had—and continued to be—deeply loved by people in my life. "But you've never been truly loved in a romantic way. Not one of the men with whom you've had an intimate relationship has ever loved you, not completely, not wholly. For them, you were never enough." And there it was. Enough. Never enough.

While that realization was painful, it paled in comparison to the follow-up: I had come to believe I was not enough for anyone, not even myself. When I looked into my past, what bubbled to the surface wasn't what I had achieved and experienced, but rather what I had squandered: opportunities, talents, and assets. I berated myself for patterns of poor judgment—staying in relationships that were terrible for me, working at poor-paying jobs offering little income and no potential for advancement, wasting what money I did have on fruitless endeavors and a frivolous lifestyle. I couldn't see the shining moments, the joys, the sheer love of life I once embraced. I had a couple choice words for myself. Loser. Failure. Over the years I established an inner

vocabulary that told myself I had not achieved anything of true significance. *Not enough.*

I needed to find a path out of my despair. I
couldn't carry on with my burden of pain. I had
taken a turn from a generally happy, positive,
fun-loving person to someone weighed down by my
very existence. Only I could fix this.

"Find a way to be enough. Nothing more, nothing less. Enough."

Perhaps I stumbled upon the best definition of
love I could find: to be enough for someone else,
and have them be enough for me. First, I needed to
be enough for myself. There was my revelation. I
had looked to so many relationships for validation,
for someone to say I was worthy of love, of compan-
ionship, of respect and, perhaps, even adoration—
which I would gladly have reciprocated. I tried my
damndest to be good enough for them, tried far
too hard when all I really needed to be was strong
enough to be myself; strong enough to recognize
when I wasn't acknowledged in the ways I needed.
I was told in numerous ways throughout the years
I wasn't enough for those boys and men to whom I
foolishly clung, and that was true. I wasn't enough
for them. I only needed to be enough for me.

Enough. A word I used so often, without much
thought. A word that suddenly became incredibly
powerful.

About this time, Sandra presented me with a
sketch by the artist Brian Andreas. It was a colorful and quirky print that I appreciated, placing
it off to the side in my upstairs office. One day,

something compelled me to carry it downstairs so it might occupy a significant place on my foyer wall. This is when I truly read the words gracing the page: *There are days I drop words of comfort on myself like falling rain & remember it is enough to be taken care of by my self.* (*Words of Comfort*, copyright 1994. StoryPeople) The words bored into my heart and soul like the healing salve I so desperately needed, helping to validate the revelations I received during my journey to define my pain. I had a pathway to joy because, after all, it was simply enough to be taken care of by my self. So simple. So true. Something I could really wrap my head around.

A resurrection occurred. Redemption was available. The smoldering discontentment within me began to fade, to rise up, seep out of me and move away, dissipating into the air around me. As the smoke cleared from that damp and stinking fire, I wiped my runny nose and bloodshot eyes, looking down instead of upward. There I found the most beautiful pair of eyes, one brown and one blue, looking up at me. All the while I'd been breaking down, Sheldon, who had trudged through his own hell, was right by my side, keeping me upright as I moved through my days. The rescued had become the rescuer. Perhaps, just perhaps, I could be enough for him.

I had a lot of work to do to get my inner compass pointing me back toward home, a process that took many months of intense soul-searching and remains an ongoing (and beautiful) journey. I immersed myself in music that inspired emotional upheaval, provided deep solace, and infused great joy, offering a kaleidoscope through which I could examine the fractured pieces of myself. Nature hikes with Sheldon, peaceful river floats, and time spent at Rivershire were my saving graces. I was reacquainting myself with, well, myself, and I heard the voice of reassurance on the breeze of every moonlit riverside night, sunny beach walk, and musk-scented woodland hike. I sought forgiveness from myself and redemption from the Universe. Healing had begun.

Fortunately I had external support in my sisters, along with a particular friend who became my sounding board. I would call him at random hours of the day or night; he always took my calls, listened to my lament, and talked me off the ledge. He knows who he is, my dear friend.

The process toward wellness provided me with a mantra that helped me cope. "I am here. I am fine. I have all that I need for this moment. It is enough. Breathe. The Universe doth provide." Real happiness and deep gratitude surfaced. I owe a great deal to this place called Rivershire. It drew unto itself two lost and wayward souls, who needed to find each other so they could, in turn, find themselves once again. I came to treasure being by myself, with my furry companion by my side. *Alone* wasn't feeling so lonely anymore.

I reassessed life as I had lived it, focusing on the experiences, friendships, joys. There was much beauty to be embraced. I replaced negative energy with positive, and resolved I would look back only for the educational purpose of self-evaluation. Then I would let it go. There is nothing to be gained by wallowing in the past. I was ready to move forward, embracing each precious moment of my life. I was ready to be simply enough.

Sometimes, If You Get Out of Bed, You Get Ham

As I made my way toward a better place, the calendar flipped to 2010. Sheldon continued retreating to the safe zone of my bed, with Snickers and Gracie joining him there often. Most nights, the four of us settled into our respective areas upon the king-sized mattress. It was good there was no man in my life, because there wouldn't have been room for him. As my pets acquainted themselves with each other, I wondered if it would always be like this, with Sheldon staying in bed most of the time. Little did I know a pleasant surprise awaited right around the corner. Ah, Easter. That day of rebirth and new beginnings.

Easter Sunday in 2010 fell on April 4, the date Dr. Martin Luther King Jr. was assassinated forty-two years prior and the same day the 7.2 magnitude Baja California Earthquake shook Mexico and southern California during the afternoon hours.

April 4 seems to produce events of seismic proportions. Even our little Rivershire world was about to be rocked.

We had recently welcomed new inhabitants into the apartment, and neighbor Jeremy suggested we celebrate Easter together. Needing the greatest amount of space available to accommodate all the attendees, it was decided we would gather in my side of the house. Jeremy's parents and sister were on the invitation list, and I looked forward to meeting them. Becki, Ronnie, Sandra (who was visiting for the weekend), and a few friends were invited, too. Everyone contributed food, and lo! we beheld a feast before us. Jeremy's mom brought a ham, plus there were yams, salads, fresh vegetables, breads, and desserts. When everyone arrived and food was placed on the tables, we sat down, sang a song of gratitude, and began filling our plates. Then Jeremy asked, "Where's Sheldon?"

"He's on the bed," I replied. "He hangs out there a lot. It's crazy, but he seems to feel safe there."

"Why," asked Jeremy's mom, "is he afraid of the cats?"

"Well, he's afraid of lots of things, and the cats do seem to unnerve him a bit. But they're on the bed with him now, so that's not really it. It's his safe zone, I guess. After all he's gone through I try not to force him to do things he doesn't want to do. He'll figure it out. He stayed with Becki and Ronnie recently and interacted really well with their dog, Bowie, so that was encouraging. It's just a matter of time."

When our meal was nearly complete, I added, "I'll go get him. This is a good opportunity for him to interact with people."

I coaxed Sheldon off the bed. "Come on, buddy. We have company today, and they want to meet you."

In typical Sheldon fashion, he sheepishly jumped down off the bed and followed me into the living room, where our guests were still gathered around the tables finishing their dessert and coffee. As was his custom upon meeting people, he sat, averted his gaze, then looked up from the corners of those beautiful bicolored eyes while raising his right paw in greeting.

The typical chorus of "Awww he's so cute!" was raised in unison, and Sheldon was showered with attention. It's unfortunate nickels didn't fall from the sky every time someone said "Awww he's so cute!", because I'd be a wealthy gal if they had. "What a sweetheart!" "What breed is he?" "How old is he?" The questions commenced as they always did when people met Sheldon. I told the nutshell version of his story for what felt like the hundredth time: "Stray on my property...built him a house...took me two years to touch him...six more months to get him into the house...etc., etc."

What happened next became yet another defining moment in Sheldon's development.

As the dishes were being cleared and removed to the kitchen for washing, Jeremy asked if he could give Sheldon a bite of ham. "Sure, just not too much. He has some intestinal issues that we're getting figured out, and too much fatty food could trigger an episode." Not the most appealing post-dinner commentary, perhaps, but I didn't want to be woken every two hours during the night by a dog having diarrhea attacks. Nights like that didn't do either of us any favors.

I also speculated that Sheldon might not even accept the tasty morsel from a stranger, especially if he was experiencing anxiety from having so many people invade his precious space. On that point, I couldn't have been more wrong.

Very gently and tenderly, but damn quickly, Sheldon snatched the piece of ham and swallowed it whole. "Wow, Sheldon, you might want to try actually tasting it for the full effect," I suggested. He wasn't listening to me. For all intents and purposes I did not even exist at that moment because, simple reasoning, I was not the one holding the ham. Jeremy's sister offered Sheldon another bite, which he also inhaled. When the deliverer of the goods moved into the kitchen to put her plate in the sink, she had a new best friend following close behind. I allowed that another bite or two wouldn't hurt, and a couple other guests jumped in for their turn at treating Sheldon, who was, literally, eating out of their hands.

I had to put a stop to the Great Ham Feast of 2010 for fear it would be followed by the Great Shit Storm of 2010, but I noticed a new confidence that I hadn't yet seen in Sheldon. It was as if a light

went on somewhere in that adorable head of his—
"If you get out of bed, sometimes, you might just
get ham."

Whatever clicked, whatever that encounter
meant to Sheldon, it was a great turning point. He
stayed out among the guests while we relaxed after
dinner. He was showered with love and attention—
not only did he not shy away or simply tolerate it,
Sheldon absorbed it with much luster and appreciation. He continued to hang out with Sandra and
me after all the guests had left, the food long put
away. He didn't return to bed that entire evening,
not until it was actually time to go there for its
intended purpose. He snuggled up atop his blanket and slept like the ham-satiated canine he was.
Better yet, the ham seemed to agree with him. No
frantic exits to the front yard occurred that night.

When I awoke the next morning, a new day
dawned brightly. Sheldon got out of bed with me
and went to the front door to be let out. When
he came back in, he followed me to the kitchen.
"Okay Sheldon, let's try something new. I'm going
to make your breakfast, I'll even tuck in a bite or
two of ham, but you need to eat in here." Sheldon
thought that plan sounded like a winner—well,
somewhat.

When I put his bowl down and walked away he
looked at me sadly, as though to say, "What, you're
not going to stay with me while I eat?" He glanced
back at the bowl and walked away, too. "I've got an
idea," I told him. "Let's put your bowl over here on
the floor by the couch. I'll sit on the couch, and you

can eat while I enjoy my coffee. Deal?" I put the bowl down on the floor, took my place on the couch and, holy cow, Sheldon began eating. Thus began our new approach to doggie dining at Rivershire.

Eventually, we got to the point where Sheldon scampered around while I prepared his meal. As I placed his bowl on the floor I said, "There you go Sheldon, eat your meat! Who wants to eat meat? Does Sheldon want to eat meat? Of course you do! Good boy!" *Eat your meat* became our mealtime chant, and Sheldon followed directions well.

However, I couldn't leave my place on the couch without Sheldon following me. Consequently, the consuming would cease until I sat back down. The combination of Sheldon's meals and my watching the *Today* show in the morning and *Wheel of Fortune* in the evening became our ritual.

There was another ritual that followed Sheldon's meat-eating episodes. When the bowl got licked clean, much excitement would ensue. "Good boy! Did you eat your meat? Of course you did! Poopy outside? Who wants to go poopy outside? Does Sheldon want to go poopy outside? Of course you do!" Sheldon's role in this spectacle was to jump about while barking wildly, spinning in circles and running for the door. When Sheldon hit the porch, he darted down the three steps to the front lawn like his tail was on fire—and yes, ladies and gentlemen, he did indeed go poopy outside. It was quite a scene.

Still, Sheldon remained a finicky and temperamental eater. He'd never be a dog that would, at will, go over to his bowl of dry food and enjoy it at his leisure, but we had made some important progress. One of my favorite comedies is the movie *What About Bob*. Like Bob, Sheldon approached his progress toward being a more confident and content creature by taking proverbial baby steps. Fine with me. It was better than taking no steps at all.

With Grace

We continued to coexist as a foursome, experiencing serenity and bliss one moment, followed by complete upheaval—usually instigated by Gracie. I am not a feline psychoanalyst, but I deemed Gracie certifiably bipolar. Frequently she went from behaving like the sweetest kitty on planet Earth straight into unleashing a monstrous tirade. The torture fell mainly on Miss Snickers, who wanted only to be left alone. It became a source of great frustration and anxiety for all of us. Sheldon retreated to the bed to avoid the fray. Snickers cowered and hissed at the sight of Gracie or did her best to stay as far from her as possible.

The side of Gracie that was gentle and loving was as dear as her monstrous side was vicious. She sensed when I was down, and she always felt it was her job to cheer me up with one of her signature hugs and a kitty kiss on the cheek. I cherished these times and loved her dearly. When she was sweet, I harbored delusions that perhaps she would grow out of her bad behaviors and stop tormenting

Snickers. Maybe she would quit peeing on all my rugs and furniture too! A girl can dream, can't she?

Gracie sealed her own fate on May 11, 2010, at 4:20 a.m. Something spooked her that neither I nor the other critters heard or sensed. We were all sound asleep, Gracie on top of me as I lay on my back, Snickers and Sheldon resting peacefully nearby on the bed. Whatever roused her did so with a vengeance. She came abruptly awake and shot across my face with back claws extended, shredding open my left cheek. Violently aroused from a dead sleep, I scrambled from my bed with my left hand pressed to my face, running for the bathroom. Horrified, I saw the damage in the mirror. Two deep, lengthy wounds glistened across my cheek. Blood ran down my face. My hand and wrist were covered in red. There was a splattered trail of blood on the floor from bed to bath.

I cleaned the wounds well, stopped the bleeding, and taped a huge gauze patch across my cheek. I returned to bed after cleaning up the trail of blood. Gracie resumed her post atop me, as though nothing had happened; the other critters also took their places and lay down to rest. I stared at the ceiling, thinking: "What if this had happened to my pet sitter? What if Gracie's claw had caught my eye? How much more of her madness can I and my furry family endure?" The answer was clear. No more.

Snickers and Sheldon deserved a safe and happy home, as did I. Sanity is priceless, and I could feel mine slipping.

For a day or two I went about my life with a large piece of gauze taped to my face. People I encountered thought I'd undergone a "procedure" of sorts. I had a "procedure" all right: a cat scan from hell. Decisions had to be made.

I weighed my options. In the end, there was only one correct choice. I couldn't bear to think of Gracie sitting in an animal shelter kennel, taken from her home for reasons she wouldn't understand. She didn't mean to harm me. It wasn't an intentional act of violence but rather the madness that permeated her mind. This highlighted the real reason I couldn't take Gracie to the animal shelter: I was not about to make her someone else's problem. That is, if anyone would even adopt her. She would not show well. Being confined to a kennel with strangers and other cats all around would bring out the worst in her.

Even simple trips to the veterinarian were feats of self-preservation—not for Gracie, but for every human nearby. On one visit, she tore my hand open with her claws after I removed her from her carrier. She then proceeded to hiss and spit at everyone in the room, the fur on her back raised. People were weighing their exit options, sizing up the others in the room, deciding who was the weakest and slowest. Who would reach the available exit doors last, to be left behind for this shrieking beast to devour? We somehow managed to get Gracie back into her carrier without anyone losing an eye, limb, or faith in God. The veterinarian assessed that the only way to examine her was if she were rendered completely unconscious. Afterward, she had to be gassed in her carrier for all of her appointments.

I loved Gracie in spite of her insanity, and I made the most heartbreaking but level-headed decision I could make. The veterinarian understood when I called and told her the story of running to my bathroom with two deep slashes across my face and a trail of blood on the bedroom floor. I explained that I needed to put Gracie down. The doctor agreed it was the right thing to do. I set an appointment for May 20, 2010. I had one week to say goodbye.

Blessedly, the day dawned bright and lovely. I needed some sunny support. I put Gracie in her carrier after many kisses, hugs, and lots of petting. I pulled into the parking lot at the veterinary hospital with a few precious minutes left before the appointment. I crouched down outside my car, looking straight in at Gracie in her carrier. She looked back at me, calm and content. I had some things I needed to say.

"I love you very much. That's why I must release you from the part of you that is tormented. Half the time, you are the most loving and intuitive cat I've ever had, and for every kitty hug you've given me I am grateful. But I'll be comforted even more by my firm belief that your sweet, loving spirit will be released to romp freely without pain, torment, and anguish. Miss Gracie, you have amazing things to accomplish. I know your sweetness will stay with me—and enough of your feistiness will remain to give you the moxie to accomplish whatever task the Universe calls you to next. You are a good kitty, and I will miss you. Please visit often, but, more than that, be free, be whole, be released. I love you, Gracie Girl."

We went inside. Lindsay, a technician at the clinic who was also one of my cat sitters, came out to greet me and show me to the room. I took one look at Lindsay and my river of tears began to flow.

Gracie was still calm, further confirmation that I was doing the right thing. She was ready to be released from her torment, too. Mild sedation was administered to ensure the euthanization went smoothly. I was ready to say farewell. I held her, telling her she was loved, as she slipped peacefully into the Great Beyond.

Fare thee well, Gracie Girl.

After she was gone we tucked her into a cardboard box lined with fleece, and I took her home. It was time for a good old-fashioned kitty wake.

No one throws a better kitty wake than I do, and this would be no exception. I poured myself a cocktail, put on some music, and gathered Snickers and Sheldon in the living room around the box containing Gracie's lifeless body, giving them the opportunity to sniff and comprehend. I'm pretty sure I caught a glimpse of Snickers doing a happy dance in the corner when she thought I wasn't looking.

I buried Gracie in the garden by the pole barn. Sheldon went along to pay his respects. He lay down nearby and watched as I placed the little box that held her body into the hole. I toasted her again and said a few more words. Cheers, Gracie Girl. Be free!

With the hole filled, I sought out a fine, large rock to place as a marker. I cut flowers and placed them there. I stood back. The kitty wake, complete with burial, was nearing a close.

Then Sheldon got up, wandered over to the spot, and stood right on her grave. "Sheldon," I said warningly, "don't even think about peeing on her." He didn't.

I dubbed May 20 the Day of Grace; the tranquil patch of land that is her resting place is called Garden of Grace. What had transpired was an act of grace, in spite of the accompanying pain and torment. Eleven days later, on my forty-ninth birthday, Becki gave me a perfectly worded tribute in the form of an original garden marker made just for us by a local artist. It read (in Becki's own words): "Garden of Grace. Where hearts seek peace and souls find rest."

Amen sista.

The Arrival of Slick and Billy

With Gracie gone, a calm fell over our home. Snickers and Sheldon began enjoying a peaceful and comfortable coexistence. It took a few days for Snickers to stop peering around corners, anticipating an unprovoked attack. When she realized Gracie was truly not coming back, she relaxed and regained her position as queen of her domain. Even though Snickers was the smaller of the two remaining pets, her sassiness coupled with Sheldon's timid nature allowed her to rule. If he was closer than she preferred, especially when his nose found its way toward her behind to get a sniff, it only took one good hiss to get him to back off. Snickers was an old girl, at least eighteen years, and it was the perfect time for her to regain control and live out her remaining days in peace. I had no plans to adopt any more pets. I didn't want to upset our own little peaceable kingdom.

Aside from the frantic enthusiasm leading up

to "going poopy outside," Sheldon's routine was rather uneventful. After clearing the porch steps, Sheldon calmly paced the yard, sniffing to find just the right spot. However, where peeing was concerned Sheldon had one very favorite place for his business. Immediately off the porch steps, to the left of the stone path, large and beautiful peonies graced the edge of a flower bed. Sheldon loved lifting his leg on these plants, which continued to grow and thrive in spite of being regularly urinated upon. I concluded that Sheldon misunderstood the flower's name; instead of peony, Sheldon heard pee-on-me. Thus, my favorite flower would be forevermore known in my world as a pee-on-me.

Once Sheldon's business was complete he calmly returned to the porch, ready to go back inside. However, one particular evening soon after Gracie passed, something moved in the twilight and caught Sheldon's attention. He bolted from the porch, barking his fool head off, something he had never done before. I couldn't see what had him so riled up, so I called for him to come back, concerned that whatever lurked in the shadows might harm him. He soon returned, a bit more puffed up than when he left. Mission accomplished. I had no idea what caused his sudden outburst.

A few days passed. Sheldon and I were relaxing on the porch during daylight hours when suddenly the same thing occurred. He left the porch in bat-out-of-hell mode, barking frantically. This time, however, I caught sight of the focus of his attention. A black cat was darting across our lawn, being chased by Sheldon. It sought and found safe haven under our back porch, the deck closest to the river. Sheldon returned to the front porch, once again proud of his protective prowess.

I looked to the heavens and said, "You cannot be serious! No, NO, NOOO! That cat is not living here." I am a sucker for a stray. I cannot let a home-less pet suffer, and I have fed many in my life. I was a tad angry with the Universe for playing on my sensitivities. "There is no way in hell that cat is living here. We just went through a great deal of turmoil to get to our current happy place, and you know it. It is completely unfair to send me another cat. Not here. No way."

Arguing with the Universe is futile. This partic-ular argument left me temporarily living under the delusion that I was not a player in the stray's wel-fare, that by stating my position out loud the black cat would simply go away. Right. Problem was, the spirit of Gracie had a little work to do. Rivershire, with its healing properties, was the perfect place on earth for a little redemption. So, Gracie sent me another cat.

It took a short while for this to settle in, but when it did, I remained resolved that this kitty would not live with us. I needed to find it a home. The little black cat was friendly, especially when served canned cat food. I was able to get close enough to pet it, and upon further review determined "it" to be a "he." A name soon followed: B.P., which stood for Back Porch, where he lived, or Black Pussy, which he was. Both worked. Coincidentally, it was the year that the BP oil spill occurred in the Gulf of Mexico. His color, combined with current events, provided the perfect nickname—Slick.

Slick had one other defining quality. He had two different-colored eyes, one yellow, one green. Two animals had wandered onto Rivershire with two different-colored eyes. What were the odds? Just another sign that this was no random occurrence. My service was required—no, it was demanded. The magnetic pull of Rivershire was at work.

Safely residing on and under my back porch with a daily food supply, Slick was lacking only one thing. He might as well have Gracie's soft, pink kitty bed. After all, she brought him here. She would want him to have it.

My determination remained firm that Slick was not staying. Before carting him off to the animal shelter, I decided to make an effort at locating his owners. Well aware there are thousands of cats who are born strays, I knew Slick probably had no real home, but he was so friendly I figured he might just have a family waiting for him to return. It was worth a try.

I went with the old school approach when attempting to reunite a lost pet with its family. I called the local newspaper. Their policy was to run a Lost/Found Pet ad free of charge for four consecutive days on any day of the week (except Sunday). I decided to start running it on Wednesday so that it would hit one weekend day.

Based upon the number of characters I was allowed (plus my desire to keep it rather vague), the ad read like this: Black Cat Found on River Rd. near Garfield. Two different-colored eyes. Friendly. To claim call Tricia at (231) 555-5555. My goal was to attract the real owner by providing some definitive details, like the bicolored eyes, without giving away too much. Some people torture and sacrifice black cats. I was not about to let that happen to Slick.

Saturday morning arrived, and I had received no calls on Slick's behalf. I knew it was a long shot, but I'd hoped for a miracle. Oh well, I tried. There was always the shelter.

It was a gorgeous June day, and I had plans for kayaking with friends on the Boardman River that afternoon. I must admit, the word kayaking, which implies skillful maneuvering of a sleek aquatic vessel, is a tad deceiving. The first kayaks we owned at Rivershire were of the inflatable variety, blow-up rafts surrounded by bumpers. They were nearly impossible to capsize and possessed the ability to bounce off riverbanks and other boats. None of the sisters had much previous kayaking experience, and inflatables seemed like a good way to find out if the activity suited us. These kayaks were easily inflated with our air compressor and even easier to deflate at the end of the float, making them convenient for loading into a trunk or hatchback. Eventually, we purchased sleeker and sturdier crafts.

For this river float only the two-person inflatable kayak was available, and I was floating solo. Taking the two-person kayak alone meant maneuvering would be a tad cumbersome, but it was double or nothing, and I took the odds. I was in the mood for a float.

Cumbersome craft aside, the outing held an added element of potential intrigue for me. I had recently met a man named Bill. Mutual friends of ours were floating that day, and I knew he might be going along.

When the group, which put in upstream from Rivershire, floated up to my house, I slid my large, yellow, fully-inflated-built-for-two kayak into the river. That's when I spotted Bill.

Bill, an accomplished kayaker, owned a couple of nice sea kayaks, but was offered the opportunity to borrow a kayak from a friend. It was waiting for Bill at the put-in spot, relieving him of the chore of bringing his own. While a kind and generous offer, Bill soon discovered the kayak was a rather unstable craft—but, there was no turning back. As I watched him float past my house he appeared to have it well under control.

It wasn't until we stopped for a little social time on the shore that Bill and I began talking. When we shoved off again we floated along together, continuing our conversation.

We fell behind the group—well, I fell behind. My big, double inflatable kayak wasn't built for speed. Plus, when I tried to hang with the group I hindered the progress of others. So I dropped back and Bill did too, asking if I minded having the company. I did not.

Bill was floating backward to make conversation easier. Coming around a wide bend in the river, we approached a spot where two pine trees leaned across the water from opposite banks, forming a narrow passage. "Um, you might want to turn around and watch what's happening ahead," I said, a bit too late. Bill spun his kayak as I plowed between the pines. Bill's kayak caught a branch and flipped, dumping him into the river. "Shit," I muttered. "Are you okay?" I called back.

"Yep, I got this," Bill replied. I tried to turn back and help, but spinning in a double inflatable kayak is no quick and easy task, nor is paddling it upstream. Fortunately, two members of our group were bringing up the rear and told me to carry on while they helped Bill dump the water from his kayak. I slowed down as best I could, and they soon caught up with me.

When we reached Shumsky Road landing, where I was taking out, Bill helped me pull my kayak from the river and load it in my car. "This has been fun," he said. "I'll call you sometime or stop by your store and see you." And with that, he got back in his kayak and floated downriver with the group to their final take-out point.

I drove the two miles home with a smile on my face. Beautiful day. Had a great float. Had fun with a nice guy. Not a bad day. It was about to get even better.

Gracie Fulfills
Her Purpose

I had some gardening to do that afternoon, but before heading out with spade in hand I checked my phone for messages. One new message, from a number I didn't recognize; what I heard upon listening to it made my heart soar. "Hi Tricia. My name is Jennifer, and I think you have my cat. I live just off Garfield, and you're on River Road near Garfield, so we're in the same neighborhood. My Arnie has two different-colored eyes. He's a big, black male cat, great mouser, neutered, very friendly. Anyway, call me. I'd really like to come over today if possible and see if it's Arnie."

Hallelujah! Praise the Lord and pass the catnip! However, I tried not to get my hopes up prematurely. She described him as big. Slick was anything but big. He was closer to scrawny. He was male. Jennifer got that part right, and I hadn't mentioned gender in the ad. The bicolored eye confirmation was a positive sign. I'd not witnessed any mousing, so I had no idea if Slick possessed that particular skill, but considering he was lost maybe that's how he survived before reaching Rivershire. Jennifer also lived nearby, another good sign.

I called her back immediately. "Hi Jennifer. This is Tricia. I just came off the river and got your message. I hope this is your cat."

"Is it okay if I come over right now?"

"Sure, but I should let you know I'm not sure this cat is Arnie. You described him as big."

"Oh yes, he's a huge cat."

"Well, if it is Arnie he's not huge anymore."

"That's possible. He's been missing since December."

"What? December? It's June!"

"I know. We figured by now he had been eaten by something or hit by a car. If it's really Arnie, it's a miracle."

Miracles happen all the time at Rivershire.

"I'm home for the rest of the day. You're welcome to come over, and I'll start looking for Slick, or Arnie. I haven't seen him yet today, but if I open a can of cat food I bet he'll appear."

"I'm on my way."

It didn't take long for Jennifer to pull in my drive. She got out of the car with a cat carrier. After a few pleasantries we went looking for the cat we hoped was Arnie, canned cat food in hand. I had been looking for him since Jennifer and I hung up, but I couldn't find him anywhere. I hoped he hadn't wandered off right when there was a chance his owner was here to take him home.

Jennifer and I walked around the house. When we got to the back porch I opened the can, and much to my delight Slick emerged from beneath the deck. He must have been hanging out in the back corner, where I couldn't spot him. He came up the steps to where his food dish and fuzzy pink bed were tucked under a patio table.

Jennifer crouched down to look closely at Slick, petting him. I could see tears in her eyes. "It's him. It's my Arnie. He's so skinny, but it's him. Hi buddy. We've missed you so much." She picked him up and gave him a big hug. He rubbed his head against her shoulder, clearly recognizing her. Arnie was on his way home after a long and diffi-cult journey, including more than a mile traveled and six months of living in elements that were at times cold, snowy, and brutal. Thank goodness for those excellent mousing skills. How else could he have survived?

Jennifer examined Arnie, discovering what I already knew. He had been in a scrape or two and was a bit beaten up, but he didn't appear to be in pain. "He's a scrapper, and I have a feeling an owl or hawk attacked him when he was outside roam-ing," Jennifer said. "He may have even been car-ried off by whatever attacked him and dropped at some point, who knows? Well Arnie, you're strictly an indoor cat now. You'll have to learn how to stay inside. I don't want to lose you again."

It's what she said next that melted my heart. Still emotional, Jennifer said, "He was my daughter's cat, and we lost her two years ago. It means the world to me to have him back."

I didn't ask how they lost their daughter—whether she died, was missing, or if they were estranged. All I knew was that Jennifer and her husband needed to get Arnie back. They needed the message and the miracle.

The blessed reunion was more confirmation of the therapeutic power of Rivershire, once again drawing to itself those in need of help, hope, and healing. The spirit of Gracie was alive and well in the moment, too, sending a message of love and redemption, letting me know that not only was she just fine, but she needed to be where she was, working her magic, making things right.

I briefly told Jennifer a condensed version of the story of Gracie and of Sheldon. She needed to know it was no fluke that Arnie came here, just as Sheldon had, lured by the draw of Rivershire. Arnie was led by the spirit of Gracie, guided to the one place she knew had a way of returning lost souls home.

Jennifer loaded Arnie into his carrier and put him in the car. "I'll need to go get some food and litter. I don't have any of that anymore," she said.

"Wait," I said, "let me give you a few things to get you started. You need to get Arnie home where he belongs. Oh, and one more thing. Please take this. Gracie would want him to have it." I handed her the pink, fuzzy bed. "Arnie really likes it."

With Arnie and his supplies loaded into the car, Jennifer and I hugged. I waved as they drove out the driveway, then walked to the porch and picked up my phone to share the good news with Mary, Sandra, and Becki. When I flipped it open to make the call, I saw the time illuminated there: 5:20 p.m., as in May 20, the day Gracie left this world. Of course that was the time. Message received. Day of Grace, indeed.

Jennifer called an hour later to tell me that Arnie was thrilled to be home. He immediately jumped up on their kitchen counter and walked to the spot where his food and water dish were previously placed, preventing the dog from getting what was rightfully Arnie's. He was ready to be served. He had earned his place at the table.

We Have a Date

Slick was out of the picture, and Sheldon was once again the Man of Rivershire—and the main (and only) man in my life. My personal introspection and exploration continued, and I found myself satiated in the most positive of ways. I was filled to the brim with a calm sense of happiness, serenity, gratitude, and love. I felt a lightness of heart and soul I had not experienced in a very long time. Great relief comes from finding a little clarity. My progress would have been impeded had I been in another relationship during the previous months. I was so at peace with being on my own that I wondered if I would ever want a full-on commitment again. Time would have to answer that question.

The summer of 2010 was flying by, as northern Michigan summers tend to do. Working at the store, floating the river, gardening at home, and spending time with sisters, friends, and my pets consumed my days. I was happy, really happy, for the first time in a long time, and Sheldon was a big part of my happiness. Snickers too, of course, but Sheldon and I were bonding in significant ways. I continued to socialize him as much as possible, with positive progress. Car rides seemed a little less frightening, and outdoor hikes were welcome adventures. We were true comrades on a learn-to-trust-again pilgrimage.

Sheldon had earned himself two nicknames: S-man, and the Amaizin' Blue Wonder Dog. I discovered that Sheldon's coloring was referred to as Blue Merle. As a huge University of Michigan fan, with its school colors of Maize and Blue, I was delighted to hear this. Sheldon was both blue and a-MAIZE-ing, therefore he became the Amaizin' Blue Wonder Dog. I don't recall how the S-man moniker got started, but it stuck. Being my little superhero, a song naturally followed, thanks to my enjoyment of Batman as a kid. Na na na na na na na S-MAN!

Toward the end of August, while I was on vacation, Bill stopped by the store to say hello and pick up some items. The employee working that day described the person who stopped by asking for me. To help me determine it was Bill, I had one question: "Did he have gorgeous blue eyes?" She confirmed that he did.

Soon thereafter, Bill sent out a group email to see if any fellow kayakers wanted to join him on a rather extensive and remote excursion to the Benjamin Islands in Canada. While intrigued, I was busy and unable to go. Plus, considering my vessel of floatation was a lifeboat-esque inflatable kayak, I knew I wasn't properly outfitted, both in the gear and ability department. I further assumed the question "Will indoor plumbing be available?" would quickly place me in the uninvited category.

I was intrigued by his adventurous spirit as well as his sense of humor. The email Bill sent out provided many good laughs. I replied, thanking him for the chuckles and asking if it was in fact he who had stopped by the store. It was. He assured me he would be in touch after he returned from the Benjamin Islands.

On the Friday following Labor Day I decided to meet some friends on the patio of a hotel located on West Grand Traverse Bay. It would be the last summer patio party, and the weather cooperated perfectly.

The patio was packed with locals. All summer we share our towns, beaches, parks, malls, roads, and every other imaginable space with tourists and summer residents. This helps boost the local economy, adding an energy to our region that would otherwise be lacking. But, Traverse City residents love those special times when the weather is nice, the town is a bit quieter, and people you actually know come out to see each other. This was one of those nights.

As luck would have it, Bill was home from kayaking and had decided to come out for a little fun, too. We spotted each other as Bill walked over to talk to a friend. "I'll be right back," Bill said. "Can I buy you a drink?" That would be lovely.

When the patio party ended, a group of friends decided to keep it going at another bar. Bill and I joined them. As the evening wound down, Bill and I made plans to attend a hockey game together during Detroit Red Wings Training Camp at Traverse City's Centre Ice Arena. Ladies and gentlemen, we have a date.

Two weeks later we enjoyed each other's company—both at the game, and afterward during lunch. Bill returned me to the rink and walked me to my car. "I'll call you," he said as he walked away. Then, he turned around and added, "I mean it, I really will." And so it began.

The Litmus Test: Good Humor, Sheldon's Approval, and Neil Young

During my months of soul-searching, I had, in an effort to avoid making poor choices where relationships were concerned, established an easy litmus test to use on a man. This, I felt, would be a simple way to weed out the incompatible male early on. One: He must have a good sense of humor. Two: He must like Neil Young. Three: Most importantly, Sheldon must like him. Sheldon had become my trusted sidekick and canine therapist. His instincts would be my guide.

True to his word, Bill did call. We had lunch together the week after the hockey game. After that, I invited him to my house for dinner. I already knew he had a great sense of humor. I learned that Bill did indeed appreciate Neil Young. Two down, one to go. It was time for Sheldon to meet Bill.

Sheldon loved Bill from the start. Litmus test complete. We may proceed.

Bill and I started spending Tuesday afternoons together on some form of excursion, including Sheldon as much as possible. Our first attempt started out a bit rocky, but it wasn't Sheldon's fault.

We took Sheldon on a hike at Brown Bridge Pond, a trail system mere minutes from Rivershire. Brown Bridge Natural Area and Brown Bridge Pond were big news in those days. The Brown Bridge Dam had been built over one hundred years prior; its construction created Brown Bridge Pond from what had once been the natural path of the Boardman River. A major effort was underway to remove the dam, drain the pond, and return the river to its original state. There was also a great deal of opposition to that plan.

Brown Bridge Natural Area is a great place for hiking with a dog. Rules are clearly posted: Dogs must be on a leash. Clean up after your pet. These rules are not always followed.

I was a stickler for keeping Sheldon on a leash when I took him places. I feared something would spook him, and he would start running. We were enjoying our beautiful fall hike when I saw them coming—three big dogs, no leashes, no humans accompanying them. They spotted us and ran toward us, hackles up, possessing an attitude of aggression. "Oh shit. Sheldon doesn't do well around groups of dogs, especially big unruly ones," I told Bill. For the record, neither do I. These three were approaching at a fast clip. My heart was racing and, apparently, Sheldon's was too.

Everything happened rather quickly. Bill picked up a big stick and I picked up Sheldon. Bill put himself between me (with Sheldon in my arms) and the onslaught. With commanding voice and the proverbial "big stick" Bill warded off the dogs, keeping them at bay. From well behind the dogs came the two women who brought them to Brown Bridge, panting and running. "Sorry," they called, to which Bill replied, "You need to get these dogs under control, because if I have to use this stick I will."

I was upset, and wanted them to realize letting dogs run amok could be problematic for others using the trail. "You're supposed to have your dogs on a leash, or at least under control so that this doesn't happen," I said.

"They wouldn't hurt you," one said, in a snide tone for which I was not in the mood.

"You know what, we don't know that," I replied. "All we see are three huge dogs running at us with no one nearby. My dog is terrified. You're responsible for keeping them under control." I had to raise my voice a bit because they and their dogs were walking away, clearly not interested in my commentary. I turned to Bill and his big stick. "I don't know what I would have done if you hadn't been here," I told him. "Those dogs would have been all over us." Our hero.

I put Sheldon down and realized the front right leg of my jeans was wet. It took a moment for me to process this, then I looked down at Sheldon. "You peed on me?" I asked him. His reply was the tipped-head-averted-eyes-raised-paw combo. His go-to stance. "I can't believe he peed on me!" Then, Bill bent down and sniffed my leg. "Yep, he peed on you alright." We started laughing uncontrollably, especially when Bill added, "If anyone is looking at us they are probably thinking: 'Did he just sniff her crotch? What an odd couple!'"

And so, with me sporting a wet leg, we proceeded on our hike.

That day, Sheldon came to comprehend that Bill was his buddy and protector. An alpha male he could trust. Whenever we went with Bill in his Tahoe, Sheldon seemed quite at ease. He sat on my lap as Bill drove, content to watch the world go by. He enjoyed our hikes and even relaxed in the back seat when we stopped somewhere that was not dog-friendly, perhaps more as a result of exhaustion than lack of anxiety, but clearly comfortable with the situation. Hanging out with Bill was, apparently, something we could both get our heads around. He was fun, funny, and great with dogs. Sheldon adored him. And, the Neil Young thing. So far, so good.

Sad Farewell:
October 29, 2010

The last weekend in October Bill and I went out of town together to attend the wedding of my friends, Scott and Colleen, in Manistee. Afterward, we headed to Grand Rapids to catch the final day of the Chihuly Glass Exhibit at Meijer Gardens. Even though we had a fun weekend of celebration planned, there was sadness in the air. On Friday, October 29, the day before we left for Manistee, Cousin Bowie died at Cherry Bend Veterinary hospital surrounded by three people he loved, and who dearly loved him: Becki, Ronnie, and Bowie's loyal pet sitter Vicki, who was working at the clinic that day.

At the time of his death the big, sweet, lovable lug was eleven years old. Bowie's health had been declining for some time. His hips frequently gave out from under him, causing him to stumble. It was clear he was in pain. He still wanted to eat anything and everything in sight, yet he kept losing weight. Becki and Ronnie took him to the veterinarian on a few occasions, leaving with some prescriptions to help Bowie feel better and cope. This day, the trip ended differently. Bowie was calm and lying restfully in the examination room. He was ready to say goodbye, or rather, until we meet again. As is so often the case, the humans involved were not ready. The doctor offered options, but conveyed these would only be a temporary fix—Bowie wasn't going to recover or stick around much longer. Becki and Ronnie made the decision to release Bowie from his earthly pain.

As Vicki later told me, "The happiest one in the room that day was Bowie." The crushing blow of loss weighed heavily upon everyone else.

Becki called me when they got home. Tentatively, I said hello. Then I heard, "He's gone."

Becki and Ronnie were devastated. The house without Bowie was too quiet and felt empty, as did their hearts. How could life move on without Bowie in it? There were only two things Becki and Ronnie weren't going to miss about Bowie. One, they wouldn't miss seeing him suffer through his pain. Two, the farting. No one was going to miss the farting. Well, maybe Sheldon. But no one else.

I would miss Bowie, too, but most of all my heart broke for Becki and Ronnie—and for Sheldon. During previous trips to Becki and Ronnie's house, the moment we crossed the light onto Zimmerman Road Sheldon's nervous agitation turned to pure excitement, and he began a little happy dance. When the dance reached its pinnacle with a doggie pirouette, Sheldon planted his paws on the passenger side armrest and created a mural of drool on the window, using his panting tongue as a paintbrush. Upon arrival, Sheldon pulled hard on his leash as he headed straight for the door to find his best buddy. Car rides were worth the trouble if it meant seeing Cousin Bowie.

It killed me to think of going over to that house without Bowie there to greet us. I imagined Sheldon exploding with happiness and anticipation in the car as we drew near. How was I supposed to explain to Sheldon that his dear canine cousin and companion, his mentor, the object of his herding efforts, his psychotherapist, was gone? I wondered if the sound of hearts breaking would be audible as we watched Sheldon search every room, finding no trace of his friend.

It had to be done. I waited until Becki and Ronnie were ready. One evening they invited me to stop by for dinner and drinks. "May I bring Sheldon?" "Yes, of course," Becki said.

Sheldon and I made the fourteen-mile drive to the blue house that once housed Cousin Bowie. True to form, Sheldon's car-riding anxiety morphed into pure joy and exhilaration as we got closer and pulled in the driveway. My heart was already crumbling.

We went inside. Sheldon was greeted warmly, as always, by Aunt Becki and Uncle Ronnie. After receiving the humans' affections, he moved on to seek out Bowie. He looked around, checked down the hall, but chose not to search the basement, likely knowing Bowie seldom went there due to his bad hips. He finally returned to the living room, where he took a moment to peer out the sliding glass doors at the deck, just in case his best buddy was lying out there. But, no matter where he went, there was no big, lovable lug to herd.

Eventually Sheldon joined me on the couch. "What do you think, buddy?" I asked him. "Your best friend isn't here. It's sad, isn't it?" Sheldon seemed to agree. He put his head on my lap for a bit, getting some loving in the form of pets and kisses. Then he got up and went over to the ottoman he so loved: his perch, his throne, his resting place in Cousin Bowie's house. He lay there near Ronnie, as if to process this information in his own personal space, while offering comfort to the grieving in his quiet and understated manner.

We sipped our cocktails and ate our dinner; then Sheldon and I went home. Never again would a trip to Becki and Ronnie's house be the same.

From Bowie to LilyBelle

Becki and Ronnie got another dog in December. Since Bowie's passing six weeks earlier, Becki had been getting messages from Bowie in the form of butterflies. She found it very comforting Bowie was visiting to let her know all was well with him in the Great Beyond.

When Bowie died, Ronnie said he wasn't getting another dog. To that Becki replied, "Well, that may be the case, but I *am*. You wanted a big, lovable Golden Retriever, and you got your wish. We both loved that dog with everything we had. He will always be missed and can never be replaced, but I've known I would want a special companion of a different kind when Bowie was gone. I want a little dog I can take places with me and hold on my lap. I'm going to start looking for one very soon." And with that, the dog search began.

Becki came across an adorable little Papillon that

was available in Ohio. What Becki didn't realize was Papillon is French for butterfly, a name given to the breed because of their ears (which resemble butterfly wings). When she figured that out, it was a done deal. Bowie had visited her yet again in the form of a butterfly of sorts, only this one had fur. Thus, on December 8, 2010, LilyBelle came to live in Traverse City with her new family. She was a little over a year old at the time.

LilyBelle was the antithesis of Bowie.

He was huge; she tiny. He inhaled his food within seconds; she barked at her bowl to announce she was preparing to eat. When she felt she had sufficiently alerted everyone to the monumental task about to ensue, she carried a few little pieces of her food into the living room, dispersing them strategically. She then consumed each tiny morsel slowly and methodically before returning to her bowl to repeat the ritual.

Bowie's energy level in recent years had diminished; LilyBelle was a spastic bundle of speed. She streaked through the house like some minuscule crazed deer, darting among people and through rungs in the basement stairway's banister. It was a sight to behold. The first time Sheldon met her he stared in stunned amazement, not even attempting to herd her. He then looked up at me, as though to say, "Seriously? What the hell is this thing, and how do we get Bowie back?" Sorry S-man. Meet your new cousin, LilyBelle.

To Herd Is
To Protect
(The Law
According
to Sheldon)

It took time, patience, and perseverance before
Sheldon truly settled into life with me and Snickers.
When it finally happened, a sense of calm reigned
at Rivershire. Snickers occupied her rightful place
as queen of her domain. She and Sheldon got along
well, and he took a cue from his big sister, becoming closer to me with each passing day. As his trust
grew, so did his confidence and intense devotion to
me.

He stayed by my side, following me wherever I
went. Sheldon was still a timid and sensitive creature, submissively averting his gaze and raising
his paw when people approached him. Which is
why what happened next took me completely by
surprise.

It began innocently enough. A contractor came

to the house, and I let him in through the front door. I watched in stunned amazement as Sheldon followed closely behind him, nipping at the man's heels. "Sheldon! Stop that," I commanded. I apologized to the man, who just laughed it off. "This cute little guy? He's harmless," he said as he squatted down, offering Sheldon the back of his hand. "May I pet you?" Sheldon assumed his usual adorable position, allowing himself to be petted.

"He must have been freaked out by your boots," I said with relief. "He's never done that before."

"Yeah, my boots can be intimidating to dogs, especially when I come into their space with their owner around," the contractor replied.

I was grateful he was so understanding and assumed this would be a one-time occurrence. I was quite wrong.

A few weeks later, a friend of Bill's named Buck and his Costa Rican wife, Roxanna, were invited to my house for dinner. I had met them previously, but this was the first time they were coming to my house. I wanted to make a good impression. The house was clean, food prepared, and bar stocked.

Our guests arrived. Bill welcomed them inside, Buck entering first with Roxanna close behind. I was on hand as well, greeting them and announcing, over the barking of the gatekeeper himself, "This is Sheldon." The usual chorus of "Awww!" and "He's so cute" resonated in the entranceway. Bill led the way toward the kitchen to pour drinks. Buck and Roxanna followed in that order as I closed the front door, turning to join them. That's when I saw Sheldon, hot on Roxanna's heels, nipping away. Roxanna, wearing shorts and colorful sandals, not work boots, was prancing and hopping about, attempting to avoid the crazed Sheltie. Bill and Buck, engrossed in their own conversation, were unaware of the commotion. In a high-pitched, nearly shrieking voice laced with her Costa Rican accent, Roxanna squealed, "Does he not like Hispanics?"

"No, no, no, that's not it at all," I said as I caught up to Sheldon and picked him up. "This is a non-racist household, pets included!" So much for a good first impression.

By this time, we had the guys' attention. "What happened?" Bill asked as he watched me head for the bedroom with Sheldon in my arms. "He was biting at me," announced Roxanna. "I believe he does not like Hispanics!"

"Roxanna, are you okay?" I asked. "I am so, so sorry! He did this once before, when a contractor came in, but I thought he was just freaked out by the guy's work boots. Bill, please make sure Roxanna is fine and get her a drink. I'm going to have a few words with Sheldon." Shit.

"Oh, she's fine," said Buck. "Aren't you, honey? That little dog couldn't hurt anyone!"

"Bill," I said again, "please make sure Roxanna is okay. I'll be right back."

We went in the bedroom. I put Sheldon down on the floor and asked him, "Now, what the hell was that all about?" Head down, eyes averted, paw raised. It was simply impossible to get mad

at Sheldon. "Okay, we need to talk. That was completely unacceptable. I'm going to leave you in here
for a while. When things calm down and we get settled in out there, I'll come back for you and we'll
try this again. I need you to be a good boy when we
have guests."

I rejoined the small gathering and discovered
everyone was fine, including Roxanna. Sheldon
hadn't actually nipped her enough to break the
skin, and I was incredibly relieved. However, as
Roxanna and the guys reveled in tales of their
recent travels and escapades, I remained perplexed
and concerned. Sheldon's behavior wasn't sitting
well with me. I had to figure out how to stop the
madness.

After we all settled in a bit I brought Sheldon
back out. He was still concerned about our guests
and showed signs of wanting to herd them both.
I think they simply moved around too much, too
quickly for Sheldon's taste. Plus, he didn't know
them. Sheldon would have preferred having Bill and
me to himself. I kept a careful eye on him, speaking his name with authority every time he even
thought about herding them. Finally he seemed
to process that not only were they not leaving, but
they seemed rather harmless. Sheldon curled up on
the floor and allowed the humans to have their fun.

I knew Sheldon's breed placed him in the herding category, but when he added people to his rep-
ertoire I began to fully understand. Sheldon took
his self-appointed role as my adoring guardian

very seriously. My furry protector knew but one approach. A Sheltie's gotta herd.

Sheldon typically refrained from herding people he knew, although once in a while even I got herded if I didn't move fast enough during the frenzy accompanying our *going poopy outside* ritual. His herding behavior usually manifested itself in a variety of scenarios: around people Sheldon didn't know, too many people in the house, or too much activity and commotion. Clearly, in these situations things got a bit too hectic for Sheldon's liking. Somebody must restore order! You cannot have people running amok, willy-nilly! It's not safe! Who better than a Sheltie to herd everyone into place?

Sheldon's herding behavior occurred only when people walked away from him. Eventually, I learned how to work with the situation whenever guests arrived. The bedroom sequester routine became the norm at Rivershire. When things settled down, I brought Sheldon out to join the gathering. It worked quite well, saving the heels and ankles of many a guest.

Speaking with Mary on the phone one night, I explained the behavior that had begun to emerge. "Sheldon?" she asked.

"Yep, Sheldon," I replied.

"Sheldon," Mary said, this time more of a statement.

"Yep, Sheldon," I repeated.

A brief pause followed. "Sheldon?" Mary said again, somewhat distrustingly.

"Yes, Mary, Sheldon!"

"Hmmm. I'll believe it when I see it," she said. My sister knows I'm not a liar, nor prone to random, unnecessary fabrications. She simply couldn't comprehend that Sheldon had it in him to behave as I described. She more readily would believe monkeys wearing hula skirts had stopped by earlier in the day to perform a traditional Hawaiian dance.

Upon her next visit, Mary was offered the perfect scenario to observe the new Sheldon. I had to work, and a contractor was scheduled to perform some repairs. Mary stayed home so that someone was available to let the repairman come inside. We speculated Sheldon's herding behavior only surfaced when I was at home; perhaps he felt compelled to protect me and me alone from perceived peril? Au contraire.

In came the contractor, out came the herding dog. "Sheldon! Bad puppy!" Mary said as she apologized to the repairman, tucking Sheldon in the bedroom. Apparently protecting Rivershire and anyone he cared about brought this behavior to the surface.

It's what started happening *outside* that presented the next challenge.

A Girl Can Dream

When Sheldon lived outside, kayakers and canoeists floating past Rivershire did not faze him in the least. He watched them pass with nary a concern. After he moved in, he was so timid that he gave passing travelers no thought. We enjoyed calm and quiet times on my front porch, taking in the sights, sounds, and scents of the wonderful world of Rivershire. Then, seemingly overnight came an unwelcome change.

Picture a pleasant summer's day. I was relaxing in the wicker couch on the porch, dog by my side, enjoying a cup of coffee in the late morning hours, when a few kayakers came into view. With that first glimpse, a low, throaty rumble emerged from Sheldon, escalating into full-fledged barking. Quicker than I could process he scrambled to his feet and fled the porch, barely touching a single step. A gray-white blur was all I saw as Sheldon raced toward the river's edge, barking his fool head off. When my brain finally engaged I leapt from my state of repose, hot on the heels of my apparently recently-possessed-by-demons canine. I'm not a good runner, but I could have been the female equivalent of Usain Bolt and not caught Sheldon. That little shit was on a mission.

Fortunately, Sheldon had no inclination toward getting wet, so he stayed on the river's bank, chasing after the kayakers in a full-fledged herding frenzy. The kayakers, however, were not concerned. "Oh, look at that little fluff ball! He's so cute!" Clearly their definition of cute and mine were, at that moment, entirely different. Appearance wise, sure. Behavior wise, not at all.

The river takes a curve at the north end of Rivershire, meandering under a River Road bridge. There is a steep rise to the road there, overgrown with trees and bramble, which, blessedly, prevented Sheldon from following the river floaters any further. Having made his point and succeeding in removing the riff-raff from the premises, he returned to me puffed up and pleased with himself—until he heard my voice. "What the hell was that? No! Bad dog. Don't ever do that again!" I suppose by now it's a moot point to mention I got the eyes-averted, raised-paw treatment. Sheldon seemed genuinely hurt that I didn't appreciate his protective prowess. Clearly he had saved us both from certain death, or at least rape and pillage. Mom clearly didn't understand that danger lurked around every corner of the property, each bend of the river.

The indoor behavior, at least, had a viable solution: put Sheldon in the bedroom until things calmed down or until the contractors finished their task. The outdoor situation proved to be more difficult. I loved being outside with Sheldon. I didn't want to put him on a tether or leash every time we ventured there. Predicting the arrival of floaters was impossible, and Sheldon typically heard them before I did. When I was lucky enough to catch the sounds of approaching floaters first, I scooped Sheldon up and held on to my writhing and barking buddy for dear life as they passed. But catching him before he began the chase was rare. Usually, I found myself apologizing to passing floaters. "Sorry! He's harmless," I'd call out to them. "He won't come in the water. Sorry!" Most people replied in the same manner: "He's so cute! What a little fluff ball! He couldn't hurt anyone."

One day I decided to construct a barrier on my smallest porch nearest the river. A few well-placed old screens and wooden signs blocked Sheldon's egress down the deck's steps. Sure, it looked like hillbillies lived at Rivershire; the only thing missing was lots of duct tape, but I didn't care. I figured I had outsmarted my smart boy. With barricade in place, I envisioned Sheldon and I hanging out together on the back porch while I relaxed, read, and sunned myself, greeting everyone who floated past as Sheldon barked frantically without escaping his new confines. It was a lovely fantasy.

The first floater to pass by experienced exactly what I just described. Barking dog, safely contained.

Grinning and gloating pet owner, waving and calling out in greeting. A beautiful thing.

Floater number two experienced the exact polar opposite. With his front paws, Sheldon put his full weight against one of the wooden signs I thought was securely wedged between deck post and railing. In one fell swoop he took it out, along with the screens and supporting braces. The result was a crashing cacophony of shoddy construction and barking dog, which served to further exacerbate the typical commotion accompanying Sheldon's assault on floaters. Added to that was the barrage of profanity flowing from my mouth in loud, rapid-fire fashion. Nice. *Welcome to Rivershire, happy floaters! A place of calm serenity with powers to soothe the savage beast.*

Mary often says I live in a dreamworld. I did indeed dream of the day when Sheldon returned to his carefree ways, unperturbed by arriving houseguests and anyone or anything passing by our home. Even the train that rode the rails on the slope across the river, with its few charming cars, became an obsession for Sheldon, sending him scrambling into action at the first rumble of its approach. I desired behavior somewhere between the dog that barely left his bed and the dog that took his S-man moniker to heart, doggie mind envisioning a giant S emblazoned on his chest: *Faster than a speeding bullet, more powerful than a locomotive, able to leap tall buildings—or rivers—in a single bound! The infant of Krypton is now the Man of Steel! S-man!* Yes, I've always been a dreamer. God help us both.

From Mary to Lary

By the summer of 2011, Jeremy, the apartment occupant who helped facilitate the Great Ham Feast of 2010, had gone. He was replaced by a single woman named Laurie, who eventually invited a friend of hers, Lary, to visit from Florida. Lary arrived at Rivershire one beautiful day in July accompanied by his canine companion, Bandit the Border Collie.

The Rivershire magnet exerts its powerful pull once again.

I was unaware that Laurie had invited company. Soon after Lary and Bandit's arrival, I heard conversation coming from the back lawn. Looking out my bedroom window I witnessed the most focused display of flippy throwing and catching I had ever seen. A closer look was required.

Sheldon and I headed outside, where Lary and I were introduced. Bandit stood approximately 30 feet away, eyes intently focused, waiting for Lary to fling the flippy, a canine-friendly plaything with a cloth center and soft outer ring designed to be thrown and retrieved. After our initial introduction, play time resumed when Lary sent the flippy airborne in Bandit's direction. Bandit shot skyward like a rocket, snagging the flippy mid-air. He ran it back to Lary and, after dropping the flippy at Lary's feet, retreated, assuming his position to wait somewhat patiently for the activity to resume again. And again. And again. And again.

I had never witnessed anything like it. Bandit's incredible leaping and catching skills, combined with his laser-like focus and intense dedication to the game, were a case study in canine OCD. The only things that mattered to Bandit were catching the flippy, then doing it again. Bandit was the doggie version of shampoo, but instead of rinse and repeat it was retrieve and repeat.

Needless to say, Bandit's behavior sent Sheldon into a herding frenzy. Sheldon was right on his heels, nipping, barking, and herding for all he was worth. When Bandit settled in to wait for the flippy to fly once again, Sheldon returned to us. As Lary wound back his arm to release the flippy, Sheldon began barking—also nipping at Lary's heels for good measure—then took off after Bandit as soon as the flippy went soaring. The moment Bandit hit the ground after snatching the floating flippy mid-air, Sheldon herded Bandit safely home. Such a spectacle as it was, Bandit seemed completely unfazed by the furry beast hot on his heels. He basically ignored Sheldon.

I deduced Bandit might be willing to play the game until he physically dropped dead from exhaustion. Fortunately, Lary's throwing arm tired before Bandit keeled over, and Bandit was forced to take a much-needed break. But give it ten minutes and Bandit was back with flippy in mouth, hoping for another round of play.

As the activity recommenced (accompanied by Sheldon's noisy herding), I asked Lary, "So, up for a visit?" "Yes," he replied, "but not sure for how long. It may be a long visit." "Oh really," I inquired. "Planning to stay for a while?" "Maybe permanently," he replied.

Lary explained he had worked many years for a restaurant chain, with several locations in Florida and throughout the country. He worked his way up to a regional management position involving long hours and few days off. Between this and his desire to get out of Florida, he was considering a move north. Originally from South Dakota, Lary had experienced cold winters and missed the change of seasons. He was ready for a slower pace of life, and the beauty of northern Michigan, with its varying seasons, appealed to him. His friend encouraged him to make the move.

A few days after I met Lary and Bandit, the pair returned to Florida. Sandra and I were unaware Laurie had not merely encouraged Lary to move north, but to move in with her as a roommate. However, when Lary pulled into our driveway one week later in a rented moving truck loaded with Bandit and all their earthly possessions, we got the hint. Initially we weren't pleased that Laurie never discussed this new arrangement with us. However, we decided Lary and Bandit should stay—as it turned out, one of the best decisions Sandra and I ever made regarding Rivershire and its inhabitants. We should have understood the decision wasn't ours to make in the first place. Rivershire knew best and continued to draw unto itself those in need of its healing energy and redemptive powers. The outside world took its toll. Rivershire helped mend the wounds.

Just as magnetic force has the power to attract, it also possesses the power to repel. The magnetic force of Rivershire behaves just as science dictates: some bodies are attracted, others repelled.

We have witnessed this happen many times over the years. Some individuals—both human and animal—arrive at Rivershire only to eventually be warded off. Rivershire knows when the time has expired on their inclusion, when their presence is no longer welcome or required. This doesn't mean these are bad individuals; they simply don't have a place here anymore. Perhaps they served their purpose or what they needed from Rivershire was fulfilled. Others needed something from this special place but lacked the capacity to receive. Rivershire tires of such inability and sends the entity packing. Comprehending this as one of Rivershire's protective powers has helped me accept that what does not belong here will be removed. I possess a deep inner peace in knowing this.

Rivershire also knows when someone is trying

to leave but desperately needs to stay. It happened once, and Rivershire held strong. The someone trying to leave was me. There was a time—when I was deep in my pain—that I thought I may need to go. My mind was so clouded with agony that I considered approaching Sandra about selling the property so I could run off to someplace where I thought the pain wouldn't exist. How do you run from what is within? You can't. Rivershire refused to let me go. The power of attraction was great. For this, I am grateful beyond words. I had many things to learn.

Of these things, perhaps the most significant has been the ability to open my mind to the possibilities the Universe provides to us beyond the physical realm. If I stop and listen to the Universe more often than the overwhelming chatter the world around me and I myself spew forth, I can expand, heal, and love more deeply. It is an ongoing process and a lofty goal. Thankfully, nature is a patient listener and profound teacher, encouraging us without hurry or judgment. All in good time.

Someday, Rivershire may repel us. Perhaps a time shall come when we've fulfilled our purpose here, when we've received what we need–enough, one might say. We can carry what we've gained here to use in another place. Others will need what Rivershire can provide. Should this time come, we will, no doubt, be made aware.

Eventually, Laurie moved elsewhere. Lary and Bandit remained. Lary quickly became more than a neighbor, even more than a good friend. Lary

became family, a trusted caretaker of our special
little spit of land along the river. With Lary's
arrival Rivershire was complete, with two humans,
two canines, and one feline. Our happy little
commune.

Lary was the perfect apartment inhabitant. He
fit all the criteria, being willing to assist with property maintenance and occasional pet sitting. As
a food industry worker, it seemed Lary wouldn't
have any trouble securing a job in the foodie town of
Traverse City. And, regarding the unusual spelling
of L-A-R-Y with only one R, not only did his name
rhyme with Mary, the original apartment dweller,
but was spelled like it, too. I took this as a very
good omen. Lary and Bandit were the newest members of the Rivershire community; our little slice
of paradise felt complete once again. Should Lary
someday move on, leaving the apartment vacant, it
would not surprise me if the new tenant was named
Gary. Or maybe Harry, but only if spelled with just
one R.

As for Bandit, he was not only obsessed with the
flippy, but also with the river, a true water-loving
beast. Fortunately, Bandit was both well-trained
and well-behaved. He did not enter the river unless
Lary allowed it. Basically, the same activity that
took place on land worked well in an aquatic setting, too. Lary stood in the river while Bandit
swam upstream. Then, once Bandit's footing was
established, he waited for Lary to release the flippy
into the moving water. Bandit swam to the flippy,

retrieved it, then paddled it back to Lary. It was poetry in fluid motion. Again and again and again. This time it was rinse, retrieve, and repeat. Lary and Bandit were right where they belonged.

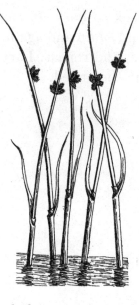

Vacation Time, Sheldon Style

Another Onekama vacation loomed on the horizon, and I really wanted to take Sheldon with me. Because of the camp's no-pet policy, I couldn't take him there. Other options around Onekama allowed pets, but were either not available for my desired dates or not in my price range. Larger, pet-friendly accommodations existed, and the cost could be shared. It was time to recruit.

Becki, Ronnie, Mary, and Jim were all going to Onekama, too. I suggested we move off-camp. As it turned out, they were interested.

Becki took up the facilities search with a vengeance. It had to offer enough in the way of beds and bathrooms to accommodate our clan. It had to allow pets. Lake access of some kind was very important. Affordability was also key.

After an extensive search for available accommodations, Becki found a match. A big, old

Michigan cottage that had been in the same family for decades sat atop a hill just off Portage Point Drive, less than a mile from camp. It had Portage Lake frontage, although we would need to traverse a steeply sloping dirt road to get there. It made for a nice healthy hike or, if feeling a bit less energetic, a quick and easy car ride. The house was spacious enough for all of us, allowing for private spaces and group gathering places; in all ways it was acceptable. Sheldon, the original inspiration for our new lodging search, was going on vacation.

As I loaded the car, I realized I was packing more stuff for the dog than for me. His food, bowls, bed, leash, harness, treats, toys, and blanket took up a good deal of space in my Subaru Impreza wagon. Plus, of course, I had to leave room for him. With the car finally loaded, we headed southwest from Rivershire. "Sheldon! We're on vacation!" I was thrilled to begin our adventure, hoping it would be the first in a series of vacations we could enjoy together. I had concerns Sheldon's anxiety would kick into high gear in a new, foreign environment. A trip just one hour away seemed a good litmus test for future vacations.

When we arrived at the house, I realized I was the one experiencing a little anxiety. I was concerned that, God forbid, Sheldon would wander off or escape the house unnoticed. Consequently his collar, with identifying dog tags, was snapped firmly in place around his neck. I vowed to watch his every venture.

I need not have worried. As it turned out, Sheldon loved vacation. He loved the house. He loved the yard, which was surrounded by woods and offered shady, grassy, wonderful spots for lying about. And no one floated by. Not one damn kayaker or canoeist or inner tube rider! Not one. This was truly vacation. There was no work to be done here. Plus, Sheldon knew everyone who joined us in the big house, therefore herding didn't seem necessary. Everyone was familiar, and moved at calm and reasonable—very vacation-like!—paces. But alas, my assumption about his herding behavior was proven wrong one night when good friends Steve and Lucie stopped by. Steve's 6-foot-plus frame did nothing to deter my short, squat, twenty-some-pound dog. Steve strolled in like he was invited and welcomed! Gads! This man must be herded! Steve either didn't notice or really didn't care that there was a Sheltie upon his heels. When everyone settled in, the herding ceased. A little work during vacation is apparently good for a Sheltie's soul.

Angel of Onekama

With that first successful vacation in the books, a storied tradition of Onekama adventures began for Sheldon and me. I wanted Sheldon to be a part of my experience in a place that means so much to me. My love of the Onekama region runs deep, all the way back to my childhood. I vacationed there for the first time when I was just three months old, and while I have no actual memories of that first experience, my innermost self absorbed the sensations around me like a sponge. My parents dipped my toes in the waters of Portage Lake and Lake Michigan. My tiny nose took in the mingled scents of pungent pine, musky earth, and deep, spring-fed water. I heard the sound a crystalline stream makes as it washes across stones within the banks of a spearmint-laced, sandy-bottomed bed in search of Portage Lake, its ultimate destination. Eventually, my little hands and feet knew the feel of the soft, wet sand that I played in for hours along the lake's reedy shores. I may have been a baby when I first experienced this haven, but isn't that when we are the most vulnerable and impressionable? My heart and soul became intrinsically bonded to that place at a time when I couldn't even pronounce the word Onekama. The Augusts of my most impressionable years—childhood, adolescence, those tumultuous teenage years—were spent in Onekama, and there I experienced all the changes of life those tender years provided. Those memories and sensations are ingrained into every fiber of my being; my annual trek to Onekama is not just a vacation but a deep-seated need. Naturally, it was important to have Sheldon join me there, to continue sharing good times, times that would become more beautiful memories set in a place that, so many years before, claimed my heart and soul—just as Sheldon had in more recent times.

And so, in August of 2012 my Subie was again loaded to the hilt with everything Sheldon and I would need for our second vacation at the beach house in Onekama. The last two packing details involved strapping my kayak to the top of the car and loading Sheldon into the front seat. The remainder of the car had so much stuff in it Sheldon wouldn't be able to jump from back to front throughout the one-hour journey, as he typically did when riding in the car. Sheldon would have to pant his way to Onekama confined to the front passenger's seat.

Becki, Ronnie, Mary, and Jim were already at

the cottage when we arrived. Mary's daughter Lori and son-in-law Jon were also there. They lived in Florida, and an escape north provided refreshing relief from the southern heat. Bill would be arriving later that evening. We were all ready to enjoy boating and beaching, eating and drinking, frivolity and laughter.

One afternoon, I was relaxing on our Portage Lake spit of a beach with Sheldon. Always the shade lover, Sheldon positioned himself behind my beach chair on a towel I had laid down just for him. We had walked down from the cottage, with Sheldon sporting his harness, collar, and leash. As we walked the tags on his collar jangled, his *dingleberries* as I called them. His natural dingleberries had been surgically removed. I felt the trade-off was a positive one. I'm not sure Sheldon agreed.

When we arrived at our beach we got settled in, and I unhooked S-man. After a time, we sauntered to the water's edge so Sheldon could cool his paws and catch a drink. I decided to take my kayak for a spin on the lake, leaving Sheldon on shore under the watchful eyes of Becki and Mary. As I shoved off Sheldon found a spot under a tree near the water where he could watch me, clearly concerned that I was floating off willy-nilly without him along to guide and protect. Several strokes into my journey, I looked back and saw he was navigating the shore, following me. "Becki! Mary! Call Sheldon!" Apparently those watchful eyes of theirs had strayed for a moment.

Upon my return to shore, my furry shadow

never left my side. He parked himself in the shade behind my beach chair, able to relax now that I had come back without drowning or cruising away forever. My true companion, whether at home or on vacation.

Which is why what happened next caught me—and all of us—completely off guard.

My friend, Jeff, stopped by our beach for a visit. As he made his way to an available beach chair, I immediately checked Sheldon to make sure no herding would occur. That's when I realized Sheldon was gone.

"Jeff, did you see a dog when you walked down here?" I asked, a definite note of panic rising in my voice.

"No, there was no dog here," he said.

"How about on the road? Did you see a dog walking along the road?" I asked, the panic in my voice increasing a notch or two.

"Not that I noticed, but I wasn't paying much attention. I was looking for your beach," Jeff said.

By this time I was darting around the yard, and had alerted Mary and Becki, who were doing the same. As they combed the yard and nearby wooded lot, keenly aware of Sheldon's love of all things shady, I ran to the road with a horrible feeling in the pit of my gut. Portage Point Drive is a relatively busy road, and I was frantic with the thought of Sheldon getting hit by a car. But—I had heard no screeching of tires, so that wasn't likely. The horror of thinking he might be lost was too much to bear. We had to find him.

I approached the road, my eyes searching frantically for any sign of him. Into view came the most welcome—yet shocking—sight. On the opposite side of the road a woman was carrying Sheldon, heading my way. "Is this your dog?" she called to me. "Yes," I replied, vast relief evident in my voice. "Oh thank God! Where did you find him?"

I crossed the road and she handed Sheldon to me. "He was walking along the road," she told me. "This is a very busy road, and I was afraid he'd get hit by a car."

I was physically shaking as I clutched Sheldon close. "Thank you so much," I said to the woman, whose name I never learned. "You have no idea. He is my world. He never, and I mean never, leaves my side. I put him on his leash to walk down here, but once we get to the beach I take it off. He always stays behind my chair. I had no idea he walked away." I felt compelled to explain to this Good Samaritan, this Angel of Onekama, that I was not an irresponsible pet owner. Sheldon's safety and well-being were my job, one I took very seriously. I was nearly sick to my stomach with the knowledge he had left my side and crossed a busy road, apparently heading for the cottage. Clearly, Sheldon was done beaching for the day. It was time to head back for an afternoon of cool, shady rest in the cottage.

I carried Sheldon back to the beach. As we approached, everyone looked up from their searching. Expressions of extreme relief greeted us, and S-man was promptly showered with loving admonishments: "Sheldon, where were you? What were you thinking? You scared us, little guy! We were worried sick. Never wander off like that again!"

I hooked him to his leash and explained to Jeff that I would be right back. Sheldon had made it abundantly clear: While he might enjoy vacation, this beach thing was definitely overrated. The cool calm and comfy enticement of the cottage was his true desire. Leash, harness, collar, and dingleberries in place, we strode up the hill.

Of course, I had a few words for him. "You scared Mom to death. Never, ever do that again. I would die a million deaths if anything happened to you. I meant it when I told that nice lady you are my world. My world! If anything happened to you, I would never forgive myself." And with that, I tucked my boy in for an afternoon nap and went back to the beach to enjoy time with family and Jeff. It took a few more minutes, and a refreshing beach beverage, to stop shaking.

Sheldon was full of surprises and certainly had a mind of his own. Each and every day offered another opportunity for him to express himself, showing sides of his character we never knew existed. My little guy was now his own little man.

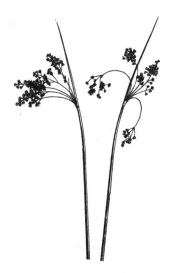

Headed to the Hole

A few months later I was preparing for another trip, this one without Sheldon. My niece, Lori, and her husband, Jon, owned a small condominium complex in Jackson Hole, Wyoming, and had invited a few people to join them there for a week. The guest list included myself and Bill, Becki and Ronnie, friends Chuck and Sue, Mary and Jim, and Sandra and her companion of several years, Eric. This generous offer was one I simply could not pass up. In all my U.S. travels I'd not yet visited Wyoming, and I was excited to explore it.

And so, on October 4, 2012, I said goodbye to Sheldon and Snickers, leaving them in the capable hands of neighbor Lary, Sandra, and Eric. Although invited, Sandra and Eric were unable to make the trek, but did visit Rivershire for the weekend. Between the three of them my pets would be sufficiently pampered.

My flight into Jackson was smooth, although I

arrived at night so I missed the spectacular view of the majestic mountains out my window as we landed. Lori and Jon picked me up at the airport and whisked me to the condo unit, a wonderful three-story structure connected by a hallway to a small lodge complete with fitness center, spa facilities, restaurant, and bar, all in the heart of Jackson Hole. The posh accommodations, combined with ideal location and overall convenience, would make for an experience grand enough to complement the Tetons just outside our door.

Sandra and Eric were not the only ones unable to head west. Bill was too busy and declined the invitation. When that decision was made, I got an idea. Cousin Ann had moved from New Jersey to Portland, Oregon, and I thought she might want to join us in Jackson. She agreed to make the drive, and was scheduled to arrive Friday afternoon. Unfortunately for Ann, she would miss the Friday morning nature tour Lori had scheduled.

At 7:00 a.m. we headed out with tour guides in two comfortable SUVs on a Grand Teton sightseeing excursion. We spotted elk and moose among other critters, but no bear. I was thrilled with the moose sighting—moose, check!—but was also determined I was going to see bear at some point. I had never seen one in the wild, and was sure if the national parks of Grand Teton and Yellowstone couldn't provide a sighting, then I may never see one (although, northern Michigan has its share of black bears). Actually, Rivershire has bears in the vicinity, and they visit on occasion, leaving behind downed bird feeders and piles of scat. Does a bear shit on my dock? Yes, yes it does. However, in all my years at Rivershire I'd never actually seen one. My desire to see a bear, especially a grizzly, was great.

After our sightseeing adventure concluded, we took a self-guided walking tour of downtown Jackson, where we connected with Ann at the Million Dollar Cowboy Bar upon her arrival. After enjoying dinner that evening at one of the area's excellent restaurants, we returned to the condo, settling in for a night of conversation and laughter before retiring. We had plans to start the next day with a visit to the National Museum of Wildlife Art, followed by a hike up to Inspiration Point along Jenny Lake. We anticipated a day filled with art, history, exercise, spectacular views, and nothing but good times and positive energy.

I dozed off, exhausted after a long, wonderful day and excited about our plans for the next. As dreams of mountains and moose filled my sleep, I couldn't possibly know how the following day, October 6, 2012, would impact my life and our beloved Rivershire. That night's sweet dreams would be my last for a while.

The River Rises

We awoke to a beautiful fall day in Jackson Hole. After a light breakfast at the condo, we headed off to the museum. I felt my phone vibrate when I was about halfway through the museum and noticed I had gotten an email from my neighbor, Dave. The subject line read, "Why we like Michigan." I wanted to read it, but for some reason the email would not open. Based on the subject line I assumed it was one of those joke emails that were popular before folks began posting such things on Facebook. I continued observing the museum's exhibits until my phone buzzed again. This time it was a call from Lary, which got my attention because Lary never called unless it was important.

At the time Lary was working at a bakery and was on the crack-of-dawn-or-even-earlier-when-no-one-in-their-right-mind-is-awake shift. Consequently, he was often home before noon. This day, he had arrived home soon after 11:00 a.m.; it was around 11:30 when he called me with definite panic in his voice. "Tricia, the river is really high.

Higher than I've ever seen it, and it appears to be rising even more."

I sat down on a bench, feeling my heart sink and my stomach clench. "How high?"

"It's up on the lawn near the small cabin," Lary said, "and we haven't had any rain. It's a beautiful, sunny fall day." There was a pause, followed by, "Oh shit. There are firemen on the bridge. I gotta go. I'll call you right back."

"Wait! Where are Sheldon, Snickers, and Bandit?" I asked.

"The dogs are with me," he said. "I'll check on Snickers. I'll call you right back."

Panic was settling into my gut with a vengeance. It was at this moment my neighbor Dave's email came to mind. Dave was not one to check in often, and he had never sent me a joke email before, so I thought it might behoove me to try and open it once again. This time it did open, the words inside making my panic level rise tenfold.

It read: *You're not at home. They just stopped to say there has been a breach at the pond. Beware that you could get a quick rise in the water level. Significant, be aware!*

My hands were clammy. My heart was racing. I frantically called Lary back and heard the words, "Tricia, I can't talk right now. The dam breached. The river is overflowing and the area is flooding. They are closing River Road. I've got to get the animals and get out of here. Now!" And with that, Lary hung up.

I called Bill, interrupting his late-morning breakfast at Centre Street Cafe, a restaurant owned by one of Bill's friends. The restaurant's owner, Pete, was sitting at Bill's table to catch up while Bill ate. When my call came in, Bill told Pete to answer for him and give me some grief. I heard, "Hello, Bill's phone." Taken completely off guard and not in a great state of mind to begin with, I managed to ask, "Who is this?" Pete, who is a wonderful, fun-loving guy and an amazing cook, began joking about how Bill was very busy and Pete was now the person in charge of screening his calls. I abruptly interrupted him. "Pete, I'm sorry but I need to talk to Bill now," I said emphatically. As Pete handed Bill the phone, I heard him say, "She doesn't think it's funny." I would owe him an apology later.

Bill came on the phone. "Yes?"

"Bill! The river is overflowing, and there's flooding at my house. I am freaking out! Lary's home; I think he's getting the animals out, but he's freaking out, too."

"Flooding?" Bill asked. "It's a gorgeous day here!"

"The dam at Brown Bridge Pond has breached! As you know, they're taking out the dam, and apparently something has gone very wrong. The pond is draining fast. I'm worried sick about Lary and the pets. And I don't know where Sandra and Eric are..." with that my shaking voice trailed off.

Bill, the consummate rock, always calm in a crisis, said, "I'm on my way. I'll get my sump pump and head out there. I'll get Sheldon and Snickers if they're there. Don't worry. I'll let you know what's going on."

I found my voice. "I'm pretty sure a sump pump isn't going to help. And, they may not let you through. River Road has been closed."

"Oh, I'll get through," Bill assured me. "I'll call you soon."

What happened next was a flurry of conversations between myself and the people with me at the museum, along with calls to Sandra and Eric and calls from Lary and Bill. True to his word, Bill talked his way through the firefighters using the premise that pets might still be on site. The emergency personnel on the bridge gave him only a few minutes to get in and get out. Water was rising all around the house. Lary was gone and so were the pets. Lary had done his job.

Sandra and Eric were at a market in Traverse City when I reached them. They immediately headed back to Rivershire but were stopped by authorities and not allowed near the house. "How the hell did Bill get through?" Sandra asked when we spoke again. "He has a way," I explained.

Phone calls continued between all involved parties. Lary, Sandra, Eric, and Bill established a rendezvous spot at a Boardman River preserve parking lot on Keystone Road. Lary had both dogs with him in the front seat, and Snickers was tucked safely in a laundry basket covered by a towel in the back seat. In the urgency of the moment, when Lary could not immediately locate Snickers's carrier, he improvised. Even though Snickers could have easily maneuvered her way out, she instead hunkered down, remaining contained inside the basket. She did not, however, remain silent. Snickers hated car rides, and she was quite skilled at loudly voicing her distress. During every vehicular excursion, her usually sweet, subdued demeanor was replaced by that of a howling banshee under intense duress, capable of emitting the most disturbing guttural wail, heralding certain death. Lary, and later Bill, experienced it firsthand.

Upon meeting, Bill took my animals with him. When he called to tell me he had them, I could hear Snickers's desperate cries from the back seat transmitted through the phone connection. "God, she makes a racket," Bill said.

"Yeah, the best thing you can do for everyone's sanity is to get her out of the car and into your house."

Bill needed pet supplies, which he hadn't had time to grab while at my house. A stop at the store was required, but I suggested Bill first take Sheldon and Snickers to his place. Both pets were upset at having been upheaved from their happy home. Sheldon was pacing all over both Bill's front seats, including across his lap, as they made their way to Bill's home.

When Sheldon's nerves kicked into high gear, he paced. Nothing caused him to pace more than a good thunderstorm. There were nights I was awoken from a sound sleep by twenty-plus pounds of fur and claws trampling all over me. Bill also

endured this. One such night, the thunder began—
and so did the pacing atop the bed. Snickers, who
was also inclined to sleep on my bed, was awoken by
Sheldon and began pacing too, not out of thunder
anxiety but rather sheer annoyance that the damn
dog had woken her. That night, I suddenly heard,
"Ow! Snickers! You stepped on my nuts!" Followed
closely by, "OW! Sheldon! Damn it buddy, now you
stepped on my nuts! You should know better, since
you at least had nuts once!"

I could only imagine, as Bill drove my pets across
Traverse City, that his nuts were once again in jeop-
ardy, and that nut-trampling wasn't conducive to
safe driving. I reiterated, "I strongly suggest you
take them to your place before going to the store."
Whether or not Bill anticipated some upcoming
nut-stomping or not, he agreed this was the best
plan.

Meanwhile, as animals were being transported,
Sandra and I stayed in touch via phone. Those of
us in Jackson Hole were still at the museum, and
I remained a nervous wreck, although my anxiety
subsided considerably when I knew the pets were
safe. But the ramifications of the situation were
bubbling up in my mind, not least of which was
potential property damage. While we were properly covered by homeowners insurance, we were
without flood insurance.

During one of my conversations with Sandra, I
leaned my forehead on a window looking out upon
a serene courtyard, a view that provided some comfort. Sandra and Eric had not yet been allowed

to return to Rivershire, and we had no information regarding the condition of our home, cabin,
and outbuildings (except for what Bill was able to
share from his brief pet-search of the property).
He snapped a few pictures, which he shared with
Sandra in person and me via text. The river was
well out of its banks in Bill's photos, surrounding
the hot tub and lapping against the sunroom, and
we knew it would rise even higher.

As I gazed out the window, Sandra tried to comfort me with the positives. All Rivershire humans
and pets were safe, which was, of course, the most
important thing. I agreed, and was overwhelm-
ingly grateful for that beautiful piece of knowledge. However, the understanding that my home
was possibly being destroyed made me nearly sick
to my stomach. As my head continued resting on
that window overlooking the courtyard, I said to
Sandra, "But we don't have flood insurance." And
with that, tears rolled down my cheeks for the first
time since I learned of the flood.

Sandra's reply helped a little. "This was a major
screw-up by the people removing the dam. This was
not an *Act of God*. This is human error, and the
people at fault will need to make things right."

I tried to believe what Sandra said. I didn't want
panic to override what was otherwise shaping up
to be a spectacular day in a most special place. The
rest of the group encouraged me to eat a little something in the museum's café, and someone handed
me a beer. All of that helped, but my guts were still

in turmoil. We returned to the condo where I continued to fret, pace, and talk on the phone. I was a bundle of anxiety, unable to calm myself completely. I needed something greater to take over. Nature was calling.

The Damn Dam Debacle of 2012, Complete with Six Otters and a Bear

Hiking to Inspiration Point was on the day's agenda. I had been on the phone so much I was low on battery power, and I needed to do something other than spend more time discussing the disaster at my house long-distance. There was nothing I could do from Wyoming. A hike up the mountain along Jenny Lake was exactly what I needed.

Heart-pounding, muscle-invigorating exercise, combined with the spectacular beauty of Grand Teton National Park, lush earth scents, warming sun, and soothing breeze, penetrated my mind, body, and spirit. I welcomed the alternative to worry and fear. A merry band of six otters swimming in Jenny Lake followed us on our trek up the mountain, providing a show for at least ten minutes. Their frivolity offered light-hearted amusement, providing a message I felt was directly intended for me: Absorb the wonder of this moment and embrace the serenity it provides.

Some of our party headed back down the trail before reaching Inspiration Point. The rest of us continued our climb and experienced a breathtaking view of the Grand Tetons. Upon returning to the mountain's base I was greeted by Becki, who was speaking with Sandra on her cell phone, explaining to Sandra that mine had died. "Here," Becki explained as she handed me the phone, "it's Sandra. She and Eric are back at the house."

Four hours after the warning went out for all to evacuate, residents were allowed to return to their properties. Sandra, Eric, Lary, and Bandit returned to Rivershire. Sandra started by saying that, at first blush, things could be much worse. Some parts of the property were a mess, others appeared to be relatively unscathed. The positioning of the cabin prevented it from much, if any, damage. High water swept across the rest of the grounds, invading the sunroom, garage, pole barn, crawl spaces, and potting shed with significant force. What the group discovered upon their return was a wet, muddy mess in each of those areas. When the water receded, silt, stench, and damaged personal property remained in its wake. Fortunately both my main living space and Lary's were elevated just high enough to avoid water rushing through those areas, which would have been devastating. Many of my neighbors, however, were not so lucky.

The true blessing of the day was that no one got killed. This was shocking, because, on a beautiful fall day, one would expect there to be floaters on the river. While there was plenty of property and environmental damage to be addressed, human lives were not lost. We were all grateful for that.

Sandra and Eric left for Ohio the day after the flood. They worked diligently during their remaining hours at the river to clean up what they could. A more professional approach would be required, and we decided it could wait until I got home. I wanted to be there to supervise. I also wanted to finish my vacation.

Bill returned the pets to Rivershire the next day. Their sleepover with him had been most pleasant. Both Snickers and Sheldon were content to lounge on either side of Bill on his couch and slept peacefully there, too. However, home was their haven, so with Lary and Bandit settled in at Rivershire, the pet-sitting arrangement resumed until I returned home.

My remaining time spent at Jackson Hole was wonderful, although there were the occasional interruptions of necessary phone calls to insurance companies, restoration services, and the like. Excursions through Grand Teton and Yellowstone certainly helped. Yet, there was a constant, nagging concern and a bubbling anger that tainted my time there. I wasn't the best person to be around, and I regret that. I wish I'd been able to completely set the incident off to the side to focus on later, but the looming concerns were a lot for me to process at the time. It was, after all, my first flood. This was new territory in the vast expanse of my life experience.

At least I did see my first bear in the wild.

The sighting occurred on a spectacular day spent in Yellowstone National Park. As Cousin Ann drove some of our group through the park, I glanced to my left and spotted a black bear alongside the road. "There's a bear!" I shrieked. Everyone looked, and Ann did her best to turn around quickly, but upon our return to the spot the bear was gone. Albeit a brief one, I could check *bear sighting in the wild* off my wish list. Not a grizzly, but a bear nonetheless.

On the Friday after the flood, I boarded a plane in Jackson Hole. Rivershire was calling, and there was much work to be done. The cleaning crew would be coming in bright and early the next day. Ahead of me were days of sorting and cleaning and discarding. More important than the stress and mess awaiting me was the fact that Sheldon and Snickers were waiting, too. Their world had also been disrupted, and they needed me. I was ready to greet them with a sense of relief like I had never experienced before. They had survived The Damn Dam Debacle of 2012—perhaps I should have had T-shirts made for them.

After a layover in Chicago, I flew to Traverse City. I wasn't exactly sure what to expect when I arrived home, although Lary had kept me apprised, assuring me it wasn't as bad as I was imagining. However, I still felt the anxiety intensify the closer I got to Rivershire.

In an ironic twist of flight paths, my plane flew directly over the former Brown Bridge Pond as we descended into Traverse City. I looked out the window at what had once been home to fish, water fowl, and a multitude of other creatures; a tranquil source of water for quenching the thirst of deer, bear, and many a woodland beast. Instead of a pond, I saw a muddy patch of land, with tree stumps sticking up from the muck and the swollen river meandering its way through an eerie landscape. It all looked so tired to me at the time; completely spent, seemingly exhausted from having retched the entirety of its guts in a matter of hours. For the second time that week I touched my forehead to a window and cried.

Rivershire took a beating and was wounded. It has taken many years to restore the property, both its natural elements and those of human creation. It also took over two years for us to receive an adequate settlement. I took a few steps backward in my state of emotional well-being during this time. I was brave through the process, but the legal battle left me drained, anxious, angry, and bereft at times. When it finally settled two years, two months, two weeks, and two days post-flood, I felt a huge weight lift from me. I could put it all behind me and allow lighter and happier things to fill my mind and time.

Even in the midst of this turmoil, there were miracles in the mix. The floodwaters flowed past the cabin without entering it in any way. The main house suffered its damage in the sunroom, crawl space, and garage, allowing us to still inhabit our home. The pole barn and potting shed stood strong, requiring only intense cleaning. Damaged items from home and outbuildings needed to be discarded but could be replaced. Several of our neighbors were not so lucky. Houses suffered devastating damage and had to be gutted entirely. Other properties were so negatively affected that their home value dropped significantly. Some people suffered injuries, great monetary loss, and intense emotional distress. It seemed as though a force field had surrounded and protected our little slice of paradise during the flood. Afterward, Rivershire assessed the damage and licked its wounds, healing itself over time while caring for and comforting its own.

Through every trial and challenge, Rivershire seems compelled to love, heal, and protect those it draws unto itself. I began to revere and respect my riverside home even more after the flood, as I received Rivershire's message of resilience. This taught me much about perseverance, faith, and belief. I can persevere through adversity, even when it feels like too much to bear. I have faith that hard times will not break me. I believe I am worthy of receiving that which the Universe wants for me, comprehending "that it is enough to be taken care of by my self." I am stronger because of where I live. For this, and the life lessons afforded me, I am forever grateful.

Goodnight Miss Snickers

The latter months of 2012 transitioned swiftly into the early days of 2013. I was in a bit of a transition myself. Sandra had acquired new business partners at the store, and my days of being the lone store manager were coming to a close. Happy to have the additional support, I was also evaluating if making my living in retail was what I truly desired. I concluded I was ready for a career change, although I would continue to be involved in the store for some time while new opportunities emerged and formulated.

The transition took several months, during which time I accepted freelance positions with Centre Ice Arena and Howe Arena, Traverse City's ice rinks. I had three years' experience selling advertising during specific events at Centre Ice on a limited basis. The new opportunity allowed me to expand upon what I had been doing, and it felt like a great fit. I still helped at the store a few days each week. Removing myself from some of the management details helped balance my schedule and my psyche, providing the symmetry I needed.

However, where transitions were concerned, another very important one was fast-approaching. It would prove to be the most difficult.

New Year's Eve and Day came and went with little fanfare. Snickers was her usual sweet self. Her weight was staying about the same, and the soft, lush quality of her fur was that of a much younger cat. There were other traits, however, that were changing. By my best estimations Snickers was between twenty and twenty-two years old, so it was not surprising to notice changes in her health and habits.

She appeared confused and disoriented at times, staring at seemingly nothing while emitting a harsh, eerie wail. When I approached her, speaking her name, she did not react. As I got closer and spoke a little louder, she would snap out of her trance, a bit startled. It seemed she had no idea anyone was even in the room. I assumed there must be hearing loss occurring as well.

During the holidays, Snickers began randomly peeing outside her litter box. For World's Best Kitty, this was completely out of character. She still used her litter box, but every once in a while she approached, looked at it, walked away, and peed on a nearby rug—or worse, the couch. I kept her boxes clean; she had two to choose from, so that no matter where she was when she needed to go a litter box was conveniently located. There was no rationale for her new behavior. I took to placing pee pads under her blankets in her favorite lounging spots around the house. Blankets I could wash. The couch, I could not.

One day, as I sat on one end of the couch and Snickers relaxed on the other end atop her blanket-and-pee-pad-combo, she stood up, stretched, looked right at me and promptly peed. She examined the spot, sniffed the area, then moved over a bit to avoid it and laid back down. My poor girl no longer had total sense of proper behavior, even her natural instinct to cover her urine failing to affect her decision-making. It appeared time to say goodbye.

It was, at least, time to make a veterinarian's appointment, which I scheduled for Wednesday, January 16, 2013.

I dreaded that day's arrival, because I knew it might be Snickers's last on this earth. I also dreaded it because I hated taking Snickers anywhere in a car. Her horrible howling was enough to make me consider driving off the road in order to put us both out of our misery.

But things would be different on this trip. When it came time to load Snickers in her carrier, she walked right in, something she had never done in her life. The ride to the veterinarian's office was calm and quiet—Snickers didn't emit a single sound. I had placed the carrier on the front passenger seat with its door facing me, something I never did. I always place pet carriers in the back seat, which I perceive to be safer than the front in case of an accident. For this trip, I wanted to talk to my sweet girl as we made the drive.

I told her she was the best kitty in the whole world and the prettiest, too. I told her how much I loved her, that if this was to be her last day on earth I would miss her—but, I would be okay. I had Snickers in my life for over eighteen years, and her absence would be difficult to bear. I told her what a good friend and companion she was. I brought up some of the adventures we'd shared together, reminding her how her antics always made me laugh. There was that time we lived in a house in the woods—back when I allowed Snickers to go outside on occasion—and the neighbor watched her scurry across the yard followed by a line of five wild turkeys. They weren't chasing her, but rather simply following behind, as though she was their leader. It must have been a sight to behold. I continued talking to her the entire way to the veterinarian's office.

Before we went inside, I pulled out my phone and took a video of Snickers looking at me from inside her carrier while I said more wonderful things to her. To this day, I've not been able to watch it.

Snickers not only typically hated car rides but also veterinary appointments. However, without exception, on this visit she was completely calm and accommodating. We removed her from her carrier. Then, the veterinarian did a brief exam, after which Snickers calmly strolled into her carrier and tucked herself in the back. "She looks pretty good for her age, and it's possible the peeing episodes are due to a urinary tract infection. Without further tests we can't be sure," the doctor told me. "We could put her on meds and see if that takes care of the problem, but there's no guarantee. You may be back in here in a few days dealing with the same situation."

I needed time to think. Snickers was content, and the doctor and her staff weren't rushing me in any way. "Take all the time you need," they told me.

Becki knew I had the appointment scheduled and asked me to keep her posted. I spoke with her on the phone, giving her the lowdown on what the veterinarian had said. "I can't decide what to do," I told her.

I spent several more minutes with Snickers in the exam room. It was nearly 5:00 p.m., and although they were being kind, the staff wasn't going to stay forever. There was a knock on the door. "Come in," I said, expecting a technician to enter, although I wondered why they were coming in from the waiting area and not from the back. Instead, Becki walked in.

"What are you doing here?" I asked.

"Is she gone?" Becki asked, without answering me.

"Nope, she's still here. She's just lying way back in her carrier."

Becki peered into the carrier. "Hello Snickers," she said. "Oh honey, you're so tired aren't you?" And with that, my decision was made. My sweet girl was old and tired. She was becoming confused, losing her sense of what constituted normal behavior. I didn't want to put her through any more tests or treatments or shove pills down her throat. Snickers was ready and so was I—even though my heart was breaking. While the veterinarian administered the shot, I petted and kissed Snickers as Becki stood by for support. In minutes, my Snicker Kitty was gone.

That evening, I tucked Snickers's body into a shoebox lined with soft flannel patterned with little black-and-white cats that resembled Miss Snickers. I placed the box on the living room floor for Sheldon to inspect. I'm not sure what animals process in this regard, but Sheldon and Snickers had become friends and companions. I wanted Sheldon to have all the information available as to why Snickers was no longer around to lie by his side or hiss at him when he sniffed her butt. One thing I knew Sheldon would miss about Snickers was cleaning up the remnants of her canned food. Sheldon had mastered the ninja-like ability of stealthily sneaking in for the clean-up kill when Snickers walked away from her plate.

Sheldon approached the box and sniffed her. "It's just you and me now, buddy," I told him. "Tonight we say goodbye to Snickers, although I know her presence will always remain here with us. But we're going to miss her, aren't we?"

Sheldon replied in his own thoughtful way by lying down beside her box and staying there while I pulled a CD from the shelf. I had nothing prepared for the wake, but, based on past experience, music, kind words, and cocktails for toasting would be involved. Plenty of cocktails.

I grabbed a random mix CD, unsure of the song list as there was nothing written on it except "Tricia's Favs." I knew, however, if it was a disc of my "favs" it might just work for the occasion. As it turned out, it worked perfectly. Every song seemed ideal for Snickers in one way or another. The mood and tempo of each changed, and I went from dancing around her and Sheldon to sitting on the floor with my face buried in S-man's fur while I wept. Sheldon was my true companion on this difficult night, providing comfort and taking in what he needed, too. We said goodbye to our sweet Snicker Kitty that evening and, like so many other things in our life, Sheldon and I did it together.

Even though it was January, it was a mild one by northern Michigan standards, and I was able to dig a grave in Garden of Grace for Snickers. I laid Snickers to rest by her formerly volatile sister with the belief that, in the Great Beyond, all are made whole. Gracie was released of her demons and restored completely to her loving, dear self. Snickers possessed those qualities in spades, with a little sassiness thrown in for good measure. Burying them together at Rivershire was the right thing to do.

I imagined Snickers and Gracie being friends in the heavens, and pictured my mom welcoming Snickers. They had always loved each other. When Mom was able, before dementia prevented her from traveling, she spent time with me up north on occasion, and she loved petting Snickers's soft coat. Snickers mirrored Mom's sweet nature, gravitating toward her whenever she visited. They were good companions.

To honor the camaraderie Snickers and Mom once shared, I wrapped Snickers's body in a jacket of Mom's I had kept after Mom passed away. I could think of no more comforting way to lay her to rest than with a little bit of Mom wrapped around her.

On a mild and pleasant January evening, Bill, Lary, Sheldon, and Bandit joined me for a graveside ceremony. I placed Snickers in the hole I had dug and asked if anyone would care to say a few words. Bill jumped right in. "Snickers, you were a very good cat. You had beautiful, soft fur. You never bit me, which was great. You were a nice cat and I liked you. You will be missed."

"Awww, that was so sweet," I said. "Thank you, Bill."

"Well, crap, I can't top that," Lary said, "so, basically ditto. I will add, however, I always enjoyed spending time with you when Tricia was away."

After I shared a few words, we toasted Snickers and the others went into the house. With Sheldon by my side, I knelt and filled the hole with soft earth, a moment reminiscent of Gracie's burial. Sheldon laid by Snickers's grave in polite repose, paying his own last respects. When my task was complete, we rose to go inside.

"Romp free, sweet girl. You were the best kitty ever." Sheldon seemed to agree.

Take Your Big-Hearted Dog and Go Home

For the first time in twenty-three years I had no litter boxes to clean. I got my first house cat in the summer of 1990, and there had been a cat or two in my life ever since.

Now Sheldon and I were on our own, and it was going to stay that way. For all that lurked in his mysterious past, coupled with the adjustments thrust upon him and the transformations he had made, I felt he deserved the least amount of disruption possible for as long as his life should last.

I also had some concerns about Sheldon's health. He coughed. It was not the first time I noticed this behavior, but it seemed to be getting worse.

When I first noticed the cough, I thought he had something stuck in his throat. It started with a hacking sound, followed by gagging; a hack-gag combo. He appeared fine and unaffected following each episode. Sheldon was due for a dental cleaning, and the veterinarian suggested the procedure might help this coughing subside, as it was possible tarter and bacteria were causing throat irritation. I scheduled an appointment.

When Sheldon and I arrived at the veterinarian's office, the doctor explained that before Sheldon was administered anesthesia for his dental cleaning, chest X-rays needed to be taken to investigate other potential issues that could be causing him to cough. Should other complications surface, putting him under anesthesia might be ill-advised. Leaving him in the very capable hands of the veterinarian and his staff, I headed over to the store. Sandra, up north on spring break, was meeting me there to help package snack mixes.

Soon after I arrived at the store, my phone rang. "Hello Tricia, it's Dr. Everett. We're not going to be able to proceed with Sheldon's dental cleaning today. Upon viewing his X-rays, I've discovered Sheldon has an enlarged heart, which means putting him under anesthesia is just too risky right now."

My own heart sank. My surroundings seemed to vanish. I felt like I was standing in a great cavern, with the words "enlarged heart" echoing off the slick, wet walls. The building could have been on fire and I am not sure I would have been able to move.

I asked, "What does that mean? What can we do?"

"Come in and pick him up. We'll discuss the situation and all the options when you get here."

"I'm on my way."

I turned to Sandra as I hung up the phone. "Sheldon has an enlarged heart," I said, my throat catching on the words.

Her response was spot-on. "We've always known that Sheldon has a big heart," she said, giving me a warm embrace. With that, I headed out the door.

I drove to the veterinarian's office in a bit of a fog, thinking the worst and hoping for the best. When I arrived I was taken into the examination room, where Dr. Everett joined me to explain Sheldon's condition. Sheldon was still in the back of the office, secure in one of the kennels. Dr. Everett put the X-ray up on the screen. I thought learning my little guy had an enlarged heart would be the most significant and shocking news of the day, but I was wrong. What Dr. Everett said next damn near took the wind out of me. In spite of all the major organs illuminated on the X-ray screen, Dr. Everett started the conversation by first pointing to a small, thin line on Sheldon's X-ray. He said with a smile, "That little line there is Sheldon's chip."

He continued speaking, moving on to the topic of Sheldon's heart, but I interrupted him. "I'm sorry, what did you say?"

He pointed again. "There's his chip. His microchip," he said, still smiling. Dr. Everett always seemed to be smiling.

"I never had him chipped," I managed to say in a small voice. Dr. Everett's smile temporarily vanished.

"You didn't?"

"No. I didn't."

Dr. Everett opened the door into the back room and spoke to one of the technicians. "Scan Sheldon," he said.

Dr. Everett returned to the X-ray screen, pointing out that Sheldon's enlarged heart was pressing on his trachea, causing him to cough and gag. "There are a few things we can do," he said, going on to explain in great detail Sheldon's wellness regimen moving forward. Medication, a new diet, and light exercise were on the list. Sheldon needed to take off a few pounds for the benefit of his heart. This, combined with heart-healthy food and heart-benefiting medications, could help him live perhaps a few more quality years, with less coughing and other related issues.

I was hearing Dr. Everett's instructions—well, sort of. I was comprehending them—well, somewhat. I kept trying to push the word "chip" from my mind and listen to the important instructions that would help my furry little man get better, but the revelation that Sheldon had a microchip currently commanded a starring role on the stage of my brain.

While Dr. Everett was explaining everything we were going to do to help with Sheldon's heart condition, a technician reached into the room and placed a piece of paper on the counter. I could not see what it said from where I was sitting. Besides, I needed to listen to Dr. Everett. "Chip! Chip! Chip!" kept repeating in my head, like some psychotic

bird pecking at my brain. "Focus!" I silently rep-
rimanded myself. "You can think about the damn
chip later."

Dr. Everett concluded his directives by asking if
I had any questions. I had a few. The first couple
involved Sheldon's quality and longevity of life
and whether or not his condition was curable. "Any
other questions?" he asked.

"Yeah. What's that?" I asked, pointing to the
piece of paper I could not read.

"That," he said as he picked it up, "is just a piece
of paper."

"What does it say?"

He showed it to me. It had a code on it, and the
name of a company associated with the microchip
inside Sheldon.

"And what does that mean?" I asked.

"Those are just a bunch of letters and numbers,"
he said. And with that, he wadded up the piece of
paper and threw it in the trash.

"Do you have any obligation to run that code and
contact the former owners?"

"If we scanned Sheldon when you first brought
him in, then I would have absolutely stressed contacting the owner. But it's been, let me see...how
many years since you found him?"

"Well, as you may recall he lived outside for two-
and-a-half years before I could get him inside, and
that was in October of 2008. He's lived inside four-
and-a-half years now. So it's been seven years since
I saw him for the first time outside my house."

"Sheldon is your dog. He loves you, and you love

him. You two have an intense bond. As far as I'm concerned, those are just numbers and letters on a piece of paper. Sheldon has been your dog for the past seven years. Nothing else has to be done at this time, or ever, if you don't want to do anything. The decision is entirely yours. If you do decide you want to contact the previous owners, let us know and we'll scan him again. Now, take your dog and go home."

Before I left the examination room, I had one more thing I needed to say. "I know what it would do to me if someone took Sheldon away from me. But what I cannot bear, what I cannot live with, is what it would do to *him* if he were taken away from me. It would kill him. He would feel so abandoned. After all he's been through, I cannot and will not let that happen."

My head was reeling as I drove home, my precious cargo with the big heart by my side. Enlarged heart. Microchip. One of those tidbits of information was enough to absorb for one day. Two was a little mind-blowing.

I struggled with the weight of knowledge that Sheldon was chipped. That bit of information was harder to process than the heart condition. I felt incredibly conflicted. At least I had an answer as to what was causing Sheldon's cough, and there were things I could do to help him. As for the chip, I pondered the responsibilities attendant to this information. Was I obligated to connect with the people that once had him in their lives? Had they been good to him? Did they deserve to know he was alive and loved? What if they wanted, demanded even, to have him returned? To what lengths might they go to get him back? These were agonizing thoughts.

The two of us being separated, especially when he needed medical attention, would be the worst possible scenario for Sheldon. His big, giant, beautiful heart would break, and I firmly believed he would die from the heartache of abandonment. The knowledge that Sheldon was microchipped offered me a new understanding of how much I loved him. Knowing there was someone out there who could prove claim to him nearly brought me to my knees. I panicked at the thought and was committed to doing anything in my power to prevent us from being separated. My job was to love him and do whatever I could to get his heart as healthy as possible. I agreed with Dr. Everett. What I saw at his office was just a piece of paper, containing mere numbers and letters. Sheldon was my dog and I was his mom. I was taking him home to Rivershire. There was no better place on earth for healing to happen.

However, Rivershire couldn't do all the work. Sheldon and I had to do our part. A new heart-healthy, weight-management diet, involving some trial and error before my finicky eater approved, was implemented. Exercise in the form of daily walks became a part of our life. His habit of chasing kayakers and floaters didn't cease with his diagnosis, and I feared these sudden bursts of exertion put undue strain on his heart. Those floating by had nary an inkling that a damaged heart lurked within the crazed, albeit adorable, fluff of fur that raced along the river's edge, barking his fool head off, followed by an equally crazed woman chasing behind in an effort to reel him in.

The speed with which he chased kayakers was an anomaly. During our walks, Sheldon traipsed along at an agonizingly slow pace before stopping to lie down, panting. "Come on, Sheldon, let's go a little further," I always encouraged. "Show the same enthusiasm you have for chasing floaters." I did not push him, however. It was clear he was struggling. We kept our walks short and sweet, just like him.

Although he tired quickly, Sheldon still felt compelled to herd the flippy-obsessed Bandit. I assumed he would eventually demonstrate his herding prowess around his cousin LilyBelle, but that didn't happen. LilyBelle was very small, all of eight pounds, with fragile, tiny features. And she was fast. No critter could circumnavigate a room more quickly than LilyBelle. Sheldon watched her zip around, making no effort to herd her. She simply seemed to perplex him.

Sheldon never bonded with either LilyBelle or Bandit the way he did with Cousin Bowie. When Cousin Bowie passed on, so did the best doggie friend that Sheldon ever had. Well, at least as far as I knew—perhaps he had close canine companions in his previous life? Little did I suspect that someday, sooner than later, I would find out.

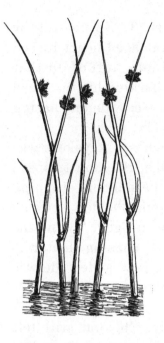

Onekama 2013: One More for the Road

The arrival of August meant heading to Onekama again. This year we stayed in a new cottage that afforded us a closer relationship with Portage Point, a delightful slip of land that juts out between Portage Lake and Lake Michigan, offering great expanses of sandy beach and two piers at the channel connecting the two lakes. Mary and Jim were unable to join us up north in the summer of 2013, so we required less space. Once again, Becki worked her magic to find a place that simultaneously fit our budget and accepted Sheldon. The location was ideal. Situated on the banks of Portage Lake, the new cottage boasted a spectacular view of the historic Portage Point Inn and was within easy walking distance of Lake Michigan.

The plan for departure involved partially loading the car Friday evening, then completing errands in Traverse City Saturday before packing the rest of our belongings and leaving for Onekama sometime during the afternoon hours. I liked to arrive in time to get unpacked before dinner; what I liked and what happened were two different things. As I scurried around Traverse City, already running later than I'd hoped, my car began jerking as the dashboard lights started to glow and flash. I limped my Subie into the dealership where I took it for service, then called Bill.

"Well, it looks like I'm not getting to Onekama today after all," I told Bill, explaining the situation with my car.

"I'm going over there anyway to take the kayak," Bill said. "Drop the keys in the after-hours slot with a note. Becki and Ronnie have a car over in Onekama. Do you really need yours there? I'll take you and Sheldon, and you'll be on vacation while they fix your car."

I gave this some thought, quickly realizing I wouldn't really need a car. I could walk to the beach. We were staying on Portage Lake, and I had my kayak. I would be able to borrow Becki and Ronnie's vehicle if necessary on those days when Bill was back in Traverse City. And, most days, I would have no need for a car. This felt like an excellent plan.

Bill picked me up at the dealership. We transferred the items already packed in my car into his Tahoe while I endured comments from Bill like, "Do you really need this much stuff?" and, "It looks like you're staying for a month."

"Guess what, Bill? There's more at home, including Sheldon and all his stuff."

At Rivershire we loaded up the rest of our vacation necessities, finishing the job by securing my kayak to the top of the Tahoe. Bill had a few more choice comments. I already missed having my own vehicle.

Finally, around 7:30, we drove toward Onekama. Bill's Tahoe, which also contained Bill's tools and gear, was now fully packed to the gills. The only spaces left were the driver's and front passenger's seats, so Sheldon had to sit on my lap. He would have anyway, but in this case he had no choice; if we strapped a rocking chair to the roof instead of a kayak we might have resembled the Clampetts of *The Beverly Hillbillies*.

We pulled into our new digs around 8:30 and unloaded the most important things, including Sheldon. I called Becki, who—along with Ronnie—was uptown finishing dinner. "You may want to hurry," Becki said. "I'm not sure how late they serve food."

"Sheldon, honey," I said, "Mom and Bill need to get something to eat. We have a new cottage this year, but just relax until we get back. It will be fine. Aunt Becki and Uncle Ronnie will be here soon. Don't be nervous." No matter my words of encouragement I knew he would be anxious and hated leaving him alone. But it had been a long day. Bill and I needed food and (perhaps more importantly) beverage.

As we drove into town we passed Becki and

Ronnie returning to the cottage. I felt better knowing Sheldon would soon have the company of people he knew.

We were enjoying a drink and waiting for our dinner when my phone rang. It was Becki.

"Well," she said, "when we got here I thought I'd let Sheldon out, in case he needed to go potty. He walked out the back door and just kept walking, turning to look at me every time I said his name, but he wouldn't come back. He just kept walking away. I told Ronnie, 'Come get Sheldon, he's going to find Tricia,' so Ronnie went outside, picked Sheldon up and brought him back in."

Fortunately, Sheldon didn't run (or walk) away too quickly. Clearly, there were no kayakers to chase along the quiet, dusty road. He strolled away at his ease, occasionally glancing back at Becki while giving her his best *not-much-of-a-tail-but-it-will-do* Eeyore-esque look, playing the sympathy card for all he was worth.

I recounted the story to Bill. "Good grief," he said. "That dog will follow you anywhere. He would go to the ends of the earth looking for you." Yes, Bill, it seems he would. Truth was, he already had.

Every morning during vacation, Sheldon and I took a morning stroll. We walked the tree-lined, quiet road by the cottage so that our path remained cool and shady, just as Sheldon liked it. Still, he was not eager for these walks and slowly trudged along despite my urging. As was the case at home we kept these constitutionals short and sweet. One day, when Bill was in Onekama, he walked along with us. "Boy, he's really slowing down, isn't he?" It was becoming noticeable to everyone.

The rest of vacation went off without a hitch. Sheldon and I spent our leisurely days lounging by Portage Lake. When I was in the mood for a brisk hike along the bluff overlooking Lake Michigan, a kayak trip on Portage Lake's tranquil waters, or an afternoon enjoying "The Big Lake's" sand, sun, and surf, I tucked Sheldon inside for a relaxing afternoon nap. He didn't attempt to wander off again, and we had a most enjoyable time together. It was a vacation I will always cherish, especially since it was the last one Sheldon and I took together.

Winding Down

Soon after our return to Rivershire from Onekama, I was offered the position of Marketing Director for Centre Ice Arena, which fit beautifully with the advertising sales I already did for the rink. This new opportunity allowed me to fully make my exit from the world of retail.

With it becoming more evident Sheldon was slowing down, and with my new work endeavor ahead of me, I said to him one day near the holidays, "Sheldon, I'm going to stay home this winter. I'm not going to take a trip to Florida or anywhere else. I've got a new job, and I just want to settle in and spend time with you. We're going to hang out here, snuggle in, and stay warm."

That was the plan. We all know what can happen to plans.

The holidays came and went, peacefully, uneventfully, and pleasantly. Bill and others asked what I wanted to do for New Year's Eve, to which I replied, "Stay home with my dog." Bill thought this sounded like an excellent plan. The three of us settled in to spend a quiet New Year's Eve at home.

We cozied up on the couch with a fire going in the woodstove, popped some corn, and put a movie in the DVD player with the goal of staying awake until midnight, so as to welcome in 2014.

Soon after we got settled, Sheldon jumped off the couch and headed for the bedroom.

"Where are you going, buddy?" Bill asked him.

"He's been doing that lately," I explained. "He goes to bed long before I do. At first I tried to encourage him to stay out here with me, but that's apparently where he wants to be. Maybe the fire makes this room too warm for him. Maybe he's tired. He just seems ready to go lie down in his bed, for whatever reason."

We were treated to Sheldon's finely honed Eeyore impression in the form of a backward glance as he left the room. Bill and I were left to ring in 2014 on our own.

With the holidays behind me, I geared up for an upcoming Chamber of Commerce networking event called Business After Hours, to be held at Centre Ice Arena on January 15, 2014. The date of the gathering was not lost on me, as it was scheduled on the eve of the first anniversary of Snickers's passing.

To the best of my knowledge the rink had never hosted Business After Hours before. I was excited to launch the new marketing packet I had created and welcome hundreds of people to tour the rink first-hand while enjoying food, beverages, networking, and prize drawings. This was "my baby"—I was in charge of planning and orchestrating every detail. It would serve as my introduction as the new Marketing Director, and I wanted to make a good impression. Thorough preparation was required.

What I was not prepared for was what happened to Sheldon and me the weekend before the event.

Sheldon started vomiting Friday evening and, naturally, did not feel like eating. I hoped that by the time we woke up Saturday he would be feeling better, but instead I woke up feeling awful, too. We both seemed to have a flu bug of some variety and took to the couch to rest. I called the vet's office, and they suggested Sheldon rest and eat only a bland diet in limited quantities, which was easy because he had no interest in eating at all. I was to monitor him.

On Sunday I felt quite a bit better, but Sheldon was experiencing diarrhea and began throwing up yellow bile. With it being a Sunday—it seems these things always happen after hours or on weekends—my only option was to take Sheldon to the twenty-four-hour pet hospital.

When we arrived, the hospital staff got us in as quickly as possible. Sheldon's weight was down, which was not shocking, considering he had not eaten much of anything since Friday. He was dehydrated, so he received a shot of fluids and anti-nausea medication. Otherwise, most of his numbers appeared normal. The veterinarian had some theories as to what might be making Sheldon sick but indicated more tests were required to determine the exact cause. Getting Sheldon hydrated and stopping the vomiting were the most pressing issues to address. Anti-nausea medications were prescribed, and I received instructions for a mild diet of lean chicken combined with rice. This, I knew, Sheldon would love—once his stomach settled enough to eat. I was instructed that he was not to have food for four hours, or water for two, in order to allow the anti-nausea medicine to take effect.

On the way home I stopped at the grocery, picking up some chicken breast and rice to cook for Sheldon. I also picked up some comfort food for myself. I was still feeling a bit under the weather, although not as bad as the day before. We both needed the remainder of our Sunday to be peaceful and restful. I was hoping for a calm and healthy Monday.

Sicker than a Dog

Sheldon and I arrived home, comfort food for both in hand. I began preparing his tasty meal in anticipation of his four-hour fasting window expiring. Even then, I was to provide only small amounts in half-hour intervals to make sure the vomiting had ceased. While I cooked, Sheldon did the best thing he could possibly do for himself: he laid down to rest and was soon snoring softly. He was exhausted from the last few days of upheaval, and there were clearly no kayakers to chase, boot heels to nip, or (quite blessedly) passing trains to reprimand. All was quiet and peaceful at Rivershire, just as we needed it to be on that lazy winter's afternoon.

My appetite was not fully restored. Still feeling rather weak, I popped in a movie, grabbed an afghan, and snuggled up on the couch. Sheldon, who was lying on the living room rug, found this to be an excellent idea. He jumped on the couch and curled up on my feet. While the movie played, we both fell deeply asleep and enjoyed that beautiful (and, in my world, rare) occurrence known as the Sunday afternoon nap.

When I awoke I felt hungry. I sat up and peeked down at Sheldon, who raised his head to look at me. "I'm very hungry, Sheldon. Are you? I hope so. It's been four hours since we saw the vet, and you need to eat something. I made you a very special meal. Let's give it a try." I warmed up a small portion of the chicken and rice, hoping he would eat and that the food would stay down.

I carried his bowl over to the usual dining spot, taking my place at the end of the couch after setting his bowl on the floor right beside me. "Eat your meat, buddy," I said, in my most cheerful and encouraging voice. Sheldon approached his bowl, took one sniff, and eat he did! He ate like a dog that hadn't eaten for the past two days. He also drank a small amount of water. I was incredibly relieved.

Keeping the food down was the next step in Sheldon's recovery. I made myself something to eat while we waited. He did not vomit, and when my dinner was ready I made him a little more of his concoction. We dined together.

We relaxed the rest of the evening, in anticipation of life going back to normal. I had plenty to do to finish preparing for Business After Hours on Wednesday evening, meaning the next few days would be busy ones.

However, that night was anything but normal. This time it was my affliction that reared its ugly head. Whatever bug had invaded my system came back with a vengeance. Everything in my system wanted out, and it wanted out NOW. I hadn't anticipated this nasty turn of events. A special cleansing occurred that night; I should have scheduled a colonoscopy for the next day. Additional prep would not have been required.

Because I was up all night, so was Sheldon. Every step I took toward the bathroom brought him out of his doggie bed. Sheldon always sensed any distress I experienced, and this was certainly distressful. Consequently, he was anxious and agitated, too. We both needed a good, solid night's sleep, but that was not what we received. It was a rough night for both of us.

Early Monday morning I called Becki. I needed supplies and was in no condition to leave the house. She came right over with the necessary provisions, leaving them on the porch for me to retrieve because she didn't want to catch whatever bug I had to give. She provided clear instructions on what to do and in what order.

The plan worked. I stopped racing to the bathroom and was getting food and beverage back into my system. Once again, Sheldon and I were exhausted; we needed another big nap. I tried to get Sheldon to eat a little more of the chicken and rice he had relished the evening before, with no success. The stressful night took away his morning appetite.

Sheldon and I hit the couch for a very, *very* rare Monday morning nap. Even though he did not care to eat, he appeared to be relaxing now that I was done sprinting to the bathroom. He again curled up on my afghan-covered feet at the end of the couch. Both completely exhausted by now, we fell into a deep and peaceful sleep.

I awoke around one in the afternoon, Sheldon and I repeating a moment from the afternoon before. Sheldon's head lifted and he peeked at me. I said, "I'm very hungry, Sheldon. Are you?"

I warmed his chicken and rice, praying that he would eat. He drank a little water, which was a great sign. I took his bowl to the usual spot and, much to my delight, watched as he ate. He cleaned up his first small portion, so I made him a little more. He ate that, too. I enjoyed canned chicken noodle soup with saltines, the old sickbed standby. Life was beginning to take a turn for the healthier.

What happened the next day truly brought great joy throughout the land—well, the land called Rivershire, that is.

I awoke the next morning feeling like a new person, having slept soundly for hours. Sheldon apparently had a similar experience. I found him peacefully lying in his bed, totally relaxed and just waking up.

Sheldon got out of his bed. "How are you feeling today, buddy? You look great, and Mom feels so much better." Sheldon was back to his old self, eagerly heading straight for the door to go out and pee. When he came back in, we headed for the kitchen. I felt well enough to start a pot of coffee; while it brewed, I made my little man his warm bowl of chicken and rice. He eagerly watched my every move, knowing a delicious breakfast was headed his way.

"What a difference a day makes, huh, Sheldon?" I sipped coffee while Sheldon ate. The joyous chorus of "Who wants to go poopy outside?" and Sheldon's exuberant barking rang throughout the house. No sound could possibly have been sweeter to my ears. Our world was back to normal.

I headed into the shower. As soon as I got good and lathered up, Sheldon commenced barking with great enthusiasm. I heard knocking on the front door, and, knowing Bill was going to stop by to drop something off, I shouted, "It's open! Come in!" I had unlocked the door for him, but the latch on it often stuck, giving the impression it was firmly locked. I kept shouting, and Sheldon kept barking. Bill, who could not hear me over Sheldon's barking, tried opening the door. Finally, assuming it was locked and that I was otherwise occupied or gone for the day, he left the bag on the porch and continued on his way.

To this day I curse that damn latch.

By the time I was able to rinse off, get out of the shower, and scamper dripping wet and towel-wrapped to the door to let Bill in, I saw only the receding tail lights of his truck. I quickly grabbed my phone, trying not to get it soaking wet, and called him.

"Hey, come back if you want. I'm here. I was in the shower. The door was unlocked, but that damn latch sticks. Sheldon was barking his fool head off, so you probably couldn't hear me yelling for you to come in."

"Nah," Bill said, "that's okay. I'll see you guys soon. I've got so much going on I need to keep moving. I left your stuff on the bench on the porch."

"Okay, well, damn it. Sheldon would have loved to see you. He's feeling so much better."

"That's great, but I'll see him later. Give him some pets for me."

"Will do. Have a great day. And remember, my event is tomorrow at the rink. I'd love it if you could be there."

"Yeah, well, I'll let you know. I hate those things. I used to go to them all the time back when I was in real estate. The old *grip and grin*. I did that for years."

It was going to be a busy day for me. A lovely one, too, although quite cold, even by January standards. The sun was shining brightly, causing the snow on the ground to glisten like diamonds. The shimmering landscape of Rivershire seemed in perfect tandem with my mood. I was happy that I felt good, and even more relieved and elated that Sheldon was very much on the mend. He needed to finish his prescription and stay on his mild diet for another day or two. The spoiling mom in me knew that if it made Sheldon happy, he would probably be getting at least a little chicken and rice in his bowl for quite some time.

I headed into town to pick up the marketing materials from the printer, then went to the rink to finish preparing the packets. It takes awhile to stuff 200 folders, and, after bending over a long conference table for hours, I slipped into the gym for some much-needed exercise. Then, I headed home.

What greeted me there was the very thing I'd been wanting to see for the past several days: my happy, healthy little guy, standing in his usual spot awaiting my entrance from the garage. "There's my good boy!" I dropped my purse and computer bag on the countertop, kneeling down to give Sheldon a big hug and lots of loving. "How's my little guy? Did you have a good day? Did you? Who had a good day?" We were back to normal. I couldn't have been happier or more relieved.

We spent a pleasant, rather uneventful Tuesday evening together. "Sheldon," I said as we got ready to tuck in for the night, "the day after tomorrow will be one year since Snickers died. It's hard to believe she's been gone a whole year, isn't it? On Thursday Mom's big event will be over, and we can pay tribute to our sweet girl. We miss her so much, don't we?"

Sheldon may have missed her, but I knew he loved being the only pet, the complete center of all the love and affection his adoring humans had to offer. If only there was more time left for him to bask in the warm glow of our adoration.

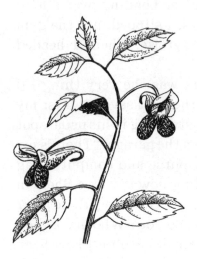

Two Steps Back

I was awoken the next morning by Sheldon pacing on the bed. As I groggily came to I said, "Sheldon, what's the matter? Is it thundering?" Then, I recalled it was January. Winter thunder is rare, although when it does occur it's referred to as thundersnow and is pretty cool. I sat up to find a very anxious Sheldon—pacing, panting. "Do you have to go outside? Let's go potty. I know it's a big day, but that's no reason for you to be nervous, buddy."

I opened the front door, but he didn't want to go out. "Come on, I'll make you your nice yummy breakfast." But, once made, he wanted nothing to do with it. Now my stress level began to rise. He panted and paced, following me everywhere in an agitated state. At one point I said, a little more harshly than I intended, "Sheldon, calm down! There's nothing wrong. There's nothing to be nervous about." He responded by sitting, eyes averted downward, paw raised, and my heart broke. I squatted down and wrapped my arms around him. "I'm sorry, buddy. Mom is so sorry. I'm a little nervous myself about tonight, and maybe that's rubbing off on you. We've had a long weekend and being sick sucks, but I think we're all better now. Life is good. Try to relax, sweetie. I'm going to get in the shower, and then I'll try feeding you again before my conference call. Just calm down, okay?"

When I got out of the shower, Sheldon was not calm. He was still panting, pacing, agitated, and not the least bit interested in eating. I got dressed and headed up to my loft office to conduct a conference call scheduled for that morning. Sheldon followed me up the stairs; once at the top he laid down, breathing heavily.

I had already called my veterinarian, giving them the rundown on Sheldon's agitation and lack of desire to eat or drink. They said I should monitor him and not give him any more medication. They understood I had an important event for work and needed to be at the rink but suggested he continue to be monitored even after I left the house. I called Lary, who assured me he would check on Sheldon throughout the afternoon and evening. He had the day off and intended to be home the rest of the day.

However, by conference call's end I knew there was no way I could leave my baby home without constant supervision. It finally started to resonate with me that this was not one of Sheldon's anxiety episodes but something different; perhaps he was still suffering from whatever ailed him over the weekend? I called the veterinarian again.

"Bring him in," the technician told me. "We have a packed schedule, but we can monitor him and treat him as needed." This, I knew, was the right decision, and I felt a sense of relief.

I lifted Sheldon into the car onto the front seat. He was weak and made no effort to jump in on his own. As we drove to the clinic, Sheldon and I had a little talk. It felt like the chats I previously had with Gracie and Snickers, but I reminded myself that I was not taking him in to be put down but rather to be healed. Sheldon sat still, panting heavily in the front seat, never even attempting to jump into the back.

I petted him the entire way to the clinic, one hand on Sheldon, one hand on the wheel. I told him how the vet was going to help him feel better. I explained that I would go set up for my event while they took care of him; I would not have to worry about him, because he would be in really good hands. I told him I loved him very much and that he should be a good boy for the doctor. I assured Sheldon I would come get him and take him home as soon as possible.

When we got to the clinic I lifted Sheldon from the passenger's seat, as jumping out of the car was also a daunting task for him in his condition. I gathered him up in my arms, realizing just how light he really felt. Clearly the illness had taken its toll.

I carried him inside, providing a bit more information to the technician who checked us in. As I handed Sheldon over to her I gave him a big kiss on the head. I said, "Mom can't cry right now because my makeup will run, and I'm trying to look good for my event later." I was trying to keep it light, even though my heart was breaking. "I love you, and I'll come get you as soon as possible." Then, to the technician, "Please, take good care of him. Let me know what's happening."

I was barely out of the parking lot when I got a call from the veterinarian's office. "Tricia, hi, it's Dr. Lint. Sheldon isn't good. His color is bad, and he is in severe distress." My stomach tightened as my hands began to shake. Dr. Lint continued, "As I understand it, you have an important event today?" With a quaver in my voice I replied, "Yes. We're hosting Business After Hours tonight at the rink, and I'm in charge of it. I'm on my way to the rink right now to set up, but I'm still close by. Should I come back?"

"No," she said. "We will inject some fluids to hydrate him, try to get his breathing back to normal. We have an air machine—actually it's an old baby incubator, with air flowing through it. It should help him breathe better and relax him. We'll monitor him closely. Give us an hour, and I'll call you back to let you know how he's doing. Go set up for your event while we attempt to stabilize him."

"Okay," I said, "but please promise me you'll call me right away if I need to come back. I'll drop everything and get there. Promise me."

"I promise," she assured me. "We'll call immediately if you need to come."

I hung up and drove in what felt like a coma all

the way to the rink. Every fiber of my being told me
to turn around and go back to the clinic, but a reasonable voice in my head spoke a bit louder, telling
me to let the professionals do what they could for
Sheldon. My being there would possibly cause him
more distress, and I'd just end up pacing the lobby
anyway, serving no good purpose. Plus, I needed to
set up for Business After Hours. Linens were being
delivered. Serving tables—and the bar—needed to
be set up in the concessions area. There were still
several hours before the event began; once everything was in place I could go back to the clinic to
see Sheldon. I had a responsibility to both Sheldon
and the rink, and Sheldon was where he needed to
be.

I got to the rink and informed Becki—not only
my sister, but also the rink's bookkeeper—of what
was going on. Her focus became the same as mine:
getting set up for the event so I could go do whatever I needed to for Sheldon. As a team, we busted
it out. Tables were set and covered with linens. One
corner of the concessions area was transformed
into a buffet-bar combo in record time. Marketing
packets and promotional materials were placed at
the entrance and around the room, showcasing the
many organizations that utilized the arena. Our
guests were set to experience a little taste of everything the rink had to offer.

An hour later, as the setup was well under way,
the veterinarian called. "Tricia, I have some good
news. Sheldon rallied after we got some fluids

and meds into him. Plus, he has responded very well to the breathing machine. He needed some good oxygen flow. His color is much better. We've had him out of the incubator. He's been walking around a bit, and we took him outside to see if he needed to go potty. This is not to say he's out of the woods, far from it. But we've made a little progress in the right direction." Relief flooded over me as the doctor went on, "We'll keep him here for the afternoon and see how he does, but he can't stay here overnight. We aren't staffed after hours, and he must be monitored. So, I know you have your event this evening. Is there someone that can pick him up and stay with him until you're done?"

I knew just the man for the job. Sheldon's best human male buddy, who also happened to desperately want an excuse for not attending Business After Hours. "Yes," I said. "I'm sure my friend Bill would be happy to come get him, take him to my house, and stay with him."

"Okay," said Dr. Lint. "Let's see how he does for the rest of the afternoon, and we'll go from here."

"Should I come see him?"

"No, we'll let you know if anything changes. Keep getting ready for tonight. We'll touch base in another hour or so."

And so, I followed doctor's orders. I relaxed a bit as Becki and I continued putting everything in place, knowing Sheldon had rallied a little. I called Bill with my request. I needed him to do something far more important than attend the event, and he

was all in. Bill would be with Sheldon while I took
care of business elsewhere. They hadn't seen each
other on Monday because of the stubborn door
latch. Bill and Sheldon could both use some big
man-little man time together, without me. It was
the ideal scenario—but, sadly, not meant to be.

Amaizin' Sad Day

My optimism following the veterinarian's initial phone call didn't last long. A second call came in an hour and a half later. "Hi Tricia, Dr. Lint again. Sheldon has taken a turn for the worse. We've done what we can to make him comfortable, and he's resting again in the incubator." Here she paused, seeming at a loss for words. I filled the silence, recalling our previous conversation about how Sheldon couldn't stay there overnight. He required monitoring, and now it seemed like he'd require more professional monitoring than either Bill or I could provide.

"Are you saying I should come get him and take him to the twenty-four-hour clinic?" I asked, breaking the quiet.

Dr. Lint found her voice. "I'm saying you should come be with him as soon as possible."

With that I left the rink, first telling Becki what I had just heard. The reality of what was happening started to sink in, along with the realization that it was happening at the worst possible time, my event looming before me.

When I arrived at the clinic, I was greeted immediately by the person working the front desk. "Hi Tricia," she said, a sad intonation in her voice imparting compassion. "The doctor wants you to go into exam room one." I entered the empty exam room with an awful, sinking feeling that I was too late, thinking he was already gone.

Soon the door into the back area of the clinic opened, and the technician stuck her head inside. "Tricia, you can come back and see Sheldon."

"Is he still, um, here?" I asked, terrified of the answer.

"Yes, he's resting in the incubator. Come on back."

I walked into the back room. There was my sweet, precious boy—my buddy, my little man, S-man, the Amaizin' Blue Wonder Dog—lying in the incubator, a plexiglass box just big enough to hold him. An apparatus was attached that gently blew air into the box, comforting him and helping him to breathe. The technician lifted the incubator's lid, then left the room so Sheldon and I could be alone together. Shrugging off my coat, I started talking to Sheldon the minute I entered the room. "There's my good boy, my sweet little S-man. Oh baby, you've had a rough day, haven't you?"

I had called Bill on the drive over and gotten his voice mail. I told him I was headed to the clinic and that, depending on Sheldon's condition, I may have to transport him to the twenty-four-hour hospital. I tried calling him again and, again, there was no answer. I left him another message. "Hey, Sheldon's not doing well. If you're anywhere near Cass Road, stop in and see your little buddy."

I walked over to the incubator where Sheldon lay and petted him gently and lovingly while I spoke words I didn't want to hear. "Baby, it's okay if you need to go. Mom's going to be just fine. I'll miss you terribly, but I'll be fine. I don't want you to suffer. If it's your time, it's your time. And that's okay. You've taken care of me and protected me long enough. Now it's time to take care of yourself."

As I spoke, Sheldon struggled to his feet. He was so weak. I wrapped my arms around him. I completely enveloped him, supporting him within the small space of the incubator while I laid my head gently down on his. "If you need to go, baby, you go," I repeated. "Mom will be fine. Cousin Bowie is waiting for you. I love you so much, and I will forever." With those words Sheldon's legs buckled, and he collapsed in my arms.

Within five minutes of my entering the room he quietly let go, finally ready because I was there to hold him. In spite of all the words I had been saying, the realization that I was supporting the entire weight of his small, soft body sent painful shock waves through me. I heard myself cry out, "Is he dying? Is he dying?"

Within seconds the technician was pushing past me to get to Sheldon as his limp body slipped from my grasp, back into the incubator. The doctor followed right behind her, stethoscope in hand. As I stepped out of the way my phone began ringing. It was Bill, and I answered. By this time I was on my knees; I had crumbled to the floor. I tried talking to Bill, but all he could make out was my sobbing. I handed my phone to the doctor and said, rather inaudibly, "Talk to him." My face was in my hands as I had, for a second or two, what felt like an out-of-body experience. Sheldon was leaving, his spirit rising, and, for just a moment, I was rising with him. I wanted to stay with him, and (perhaps) Sheldon wanted me to come along.

I heard the doctor quickly explain to Bill that Sheldon was passing, and could he come? Then she hung up. I heard her soft words as she lifted Sheldon from inside the incubator, placing him onto the metal examination table. "Tricia, you should come be with Sheldon."

Those words brought me, literally, back to earth. This was another journey Sheldon would take without me. I was to remain here.

As I began rising to my feet, I had a few stern words with myself: "Get up and get it together right now! Sheldon deserves better than you sniveling on the floor."

I went to him and wrapped him in my arms again. He was mostly gone, but that sweet, loving, big, big heart of his still had a few beats left. The doctor held the stethoscope to him, and finally, after I spoke more love-soaked words to my little man about being the best doggie in the whole wide world, saying how much I loved him and always would, Dr. Lint said, "He's gone."

I buried my face in his fur and—resigning myself to sorrow and loss—wept more tears.

Sheldon had waited for me. Twice. First, he waited for me to get to the clinic so I could hold him as his spirit soared. Then, his beating heart waited just a little bit longer for me to come back to reality and fully accept that it was his time to go. He died in my arms, exactly how we both needed it to be.

I Need to Know

I took a deep breath and released Sheldon, drained of tears at last. For a while we stood around him and talked. "I've seen it happen a few times," the doctor told me. "A pet waits for their owner to arrive, and within minutes they die. It happens especially with those pets that have a deep connection to their people. You and Sheldon shared a special bond. He waited for you to get here."

My little man, who always had to be right by my side while living, felt the same way about dying. I imagined him saying, "I need to have Mom here. I need to make sure she's okay. I need to be right by her side when I go."

Also typical of Sheldon was his timing. In his manner of always looking out for me, he managed it perfectly. I again had a sense of how Sheldon might put it into words: "Mom has her big event tonight. I need to leave today, but if I time it right she can get everything set up, come be with me, then get back. It's very important."

The doctor and some of her team remained around Sheldon, sharing stories about his last few hours at the clinic. The best story was that at one point, when he was doing pretty well, they removed him from the incubator so he could walk around. They took him outside to relieve himself, but he didn't go. Sheldon was allowed to continue strolling around in the back room of the clinic, where he discovered a large kennel with an open door and a nice soft bed with blankets. This is where Rennie the Office Cat slept at night when the clinic was closed. Sheldon sniffed inside and, for a moment, the staff thought he might go inside and lie down, but instead Sheldon lifted his leg and peed on the blankets. We all got a major chuckle out of that. "Take that, Rennie the Office Cat. Now you have a little S-man scent on your bed."

The door from the waiting room opened. I knew Bill was not stopping by; he'd explained to the doctor that he was in the midst of a plumbing predicament at his sister's house, which involved a major leak. To leave at the time of my call would mean abandoning a potential disaster in progress, and that was just not possible. Instead Becki walked in, just like she had when Snickers and I were preparing to say goodbye a mere 364 days earlier.

"Is he gone?" she asked. She then saw Sheldon on the table, not needing my reply to have her answer. Becki went over to him and said goodbye.

I was not ready to leave the clinic, even though by now it was past closing time. The wonderful staff did not push me in any way. "Just take your time," they told me. "Say your goodbyes."

I made the decision to have him cremated. When Snickers died the year prior, January's weather had been mild by northern Michigan standards. A year later and it was just the opposite: very cold, with a good amount of snow on the ground and more falling from the sky. There was no way I could bury Sheldon. My unwillingness to leave stemmed not only from the realization that, once I left the room, I would never see his sweet face or touch his soft fur ever again, but also because I had one more important matter to address.

"Dr. Lint," I said, "I'm not sure if Dr. Everett ever told you, but we recently discovered that Sheldon has a chip. I want to have him scanned."

Dr. Lint told me she was aware. The information was in Sheldon's file. A wand-like device was brought into the room and waved across his body. When they had a reading, they went in the back to see if the code would reveal answers about Sheldon's previous life. The technician returned momentarily, handing me a yellow lined sheet of paper bearing Sheldon's official time of death— 4:24 p.m.—along with a code. Under the code were written these words: Sheltie Blue Merle, Franklin Park, IL. This was followed by 2003, the year he was chipped, along with a name, street address, phone number, and an alternate contact's name and phone number.

"Franklin Park, Illinois," I wondered out loud. "How the hell did he get up here?"

"Well," said Dr. Lint, "when and if you're ever ready to find out, the place to start is right there in your hands."

The staff went into other reaches of the clinic to close up for the day. Becki and I stood by Sheldon's body for a bit longer. Of course he was gone, yet his physical being still lay in front of me. It was tough for me to walk away from my sweet little man, knowing I would never see him again. The hardest part of my parents' funerals was when it came time to close their caskets. There is a finality in that last glimpse that gives me great pause. As difficult as it was, I had to walk away.

We took a few more moments to touch Sheldon and say a final goodbye. Then, Becki and I walked from the room, but not before I glanced back one more time. Goodbye, sweet boy. Happy trails, S-man. Romp freely and be whole once again.

Enough Love

Becki and I parted ways in the parking lot. She was headed to dinner with a friend before a comedy show they were attending. "Are you going home or to the rink?" she asked. "You could always come with us to dinner, and maybe we can get another ticket to the show."

"I appreciate the offer but, no, I'm going to the rink. I need to be there. I can't even begin to think about going home to an empty house right now."

The event had already begun; it was now after five o'clock. The brief speeches and prize drawings were to be held at 6:15. Even though we had backup in place for someone else to speak if I was unable to return, I felt strongly it should be me delivering the message I had been so diligently rehearsing.

As I drove to the rink, I called Bill to let him know I was now composed and doing okay for the moment. I also told him about the information on the yellow sheet of paper.

"Franklin Park, Illinois," he asked. "Really?"

"Yes. Interesting, isn't it?"

"Good luck at your event. I won't be there. Chris has a major plumbing problem here at her house that I've almost got resolved, but I'll come to your place later. Let me know when you're headed home."

I hung up the phone as I pulled into the rink's parking lot. Time to go to work.

I was greeted warmly by everyone who knew what had happened and worked the crowd with what I hoped was masked cheerfulness, greeting those I knew and introducing myself to those I didn't. When my time arrived to say a few words, everything I'd rehearsed came back with ease and spilled from my mouth as though nothing else of any importance was going on in my head. After I finished, I moved toward the exit to make sure everyone leaving had received a marketing packet and was bid a proper farewell. My "big event" rapidly came to a close; it appeared everyone had had a good time. By any measuring stick, a success.

I started to help clean up, but the rink's executive director stopped me. "We've got plenty of crew on hand for that tonight. You get out of here. Great event. Thank you for all your hard work. I don't want to see you back here until Monday."

With that, I gathered my things, put on my coat, and left the building with one of the volunteers. We made small talk as we went down the stairs and out into the cold, crisp, snowy night. She went toward her car and I toward mine, in opposite directions.

Two steps off of the sidewalk, alone in the cold, dark night, I felt the rush of what had been lying dormant within me come crashing forward like the Boardman River on the day of the flood. I was instantly sobbing once again.

As I strode the rest of the way to my car, I asked aloud to no one in particular through heaving sobs: "Can someone explain to me how I'm supposed to walk into that house? How am I supposed to go home without Sheldon there to greet me? How? Because I have no fucking idea how to do that." I sat down into my car, crying, hoping the dark night might provide an answer.

I called Bill to let him know I was heading home. When he answered, he heard the same words through choked sobs: "Can you please explain to me how I'm supposed to go home and walk into that house without Sheldon there?"

"I'm on my way," said Bill. "I'll be there in fifteen minutes. And, I'm bringing dinner."

I knew I would arrive home before Bill could get there, and the thought of walking in alone remained daunting. I called someone whom I knew would be able to relate. My friend Pat once had a dog named Wolfie, an American Eskimo about the same size as Sheldon. Pat and Wolfie were true companions, just like Sheldon and me. When, a few years back, Wolfie became too sick to continue living his exuberant life, Pat had decided to put him down, and she still missed him dearly. She would be able to understand my pain. The news would hurt Pat, too; she had known and loved Sheldon.

By the time I reached Pat, I had stopped crying. Pat took my place. While I drove and told her all that had happened, she wept. When I pulled into my garage Pat stayed on the line, saying, "Just keep talking to me. Remember, I had to walk into my empty house after Wolfie died, so I know how hard that is. At least this way, you'll have someone walking in with you."

I went inside. There was no sweet, loving bundle of fur to greet me in the usual spot. No happy doggie to jump up on my legs to get pets and kisses. There was only stillness, silence—save for Pat's voice on the phone.

Pat and I continued talking until I heard Bill walk in. It was a relief to have my dear companion in the house to love and embrace me during this sad time. Bill, too, was grieving. He had loved Sheldon very much.

Bill made us some cocktails, and we toasted Sheldon. Over and over, Bill repeated, for no apparent reason, "That little guy" in the most sweet, tender way. They were such good buddies. Bill started a fire in the woodstove and made a wonderful pot of soup, the perfect combination for heartbroken friends on a cold, sad winter's night. At one point, while Bill was stirring the pot of soup, I asked him something that was weighing heavily on me at that moment.

"Bill, did I love him enough?"

Bill—thinking he hadn't heard correctly—turned around to look at me. "What did you say?"

"Did I love him enough?" I repeated.

There was that word again: enough. Had I been enough for Sheldon?

"Are you kidding me? You can't be serious," Bill said, coming over to give me a big hug. "I have never seen anyone love a dog as much as you loved Sheldon. And I've never seen a dog love someone as much as he loved you. You can't seriously be asking me this. That little guy!"

Those words meant the world to me, as did Bill's caring gesture of offering a simple meal, which we shared by the fire. I was terribly sad—we both were—but a calming energy began to emerge.

Yes, I loved him enough. And, I was enough for Sheldon. True love exists in many forms.

We went to bed and, blessedly, fell asleep. I was unsure if I would be able to sleep, but I was so physically and emotionally exhausted the question got answered as soon as my head hit the pillow. I awoke around 3:00 a.m. and realized Bill was awake, too. It felt strange, knowing Sheldon was not tucked into his bed at the foot of mine. I was pet-less for the first time in twenty-some years. The abruptness of that reality was hard to process.

Bill and I laid awake for a while, sharing stories about Sheldon. We started to laugh. There were so many funny Sheldon stories: when he peed on my leg the day we were surrounded by big dogs on our hike, his exuberance for "going poopy outside," how he lost his ever-lovin' mind every time the train went by, his maniacal chasing of kayakers and, of course, the night Sheldon went nipping at Roxanna's heels as she shrieked, "Does he not like Hispanics?" All brought laughter and warm thoughts in the middle of the dark night. There would be no replacing Sheldon, but we would always have our memories.

From the first time I saw Sheldon I shed many tears over him, but the everlasting smile on my face and in my heart will never fade. I am richer for having had him in my life. He changed my perspective on life—on my very approach to living—in powerful and significant ways. The process of encouraging Sheldon to find the means to survive and trust again, to settle into his most authentic self—even those parts that I found frustrating—allowed me to gain a better understanding of compassion. This lesson translated to how I related to others and—perhaps most significantly—myself. I am who I am. Yes, I can better myself, but I can also embrace those messy parts of myself that make me, me. Sheldon challenged me and I him. We grew in experience and ability together. And we loved each other enough, just as we were. Any heartache I felt during the eight years I had Sheldon in my life paled in comparison to the sheer joy of loving him. My heart, too, had enlarged with the experience.

Hallowed Ground

The next day was rough, and I knew the weekend would be, too. Bill agreed to stay over every night through the weekend, just in case it became unbearable for me to be home alone. I had a previously scheduled meeting for Thursday morning, and even though my boss told me to stay away from work until Monday, it was easier to go out than be alone in my empty house.

Thursday was January 16, 2014, exactly one year since Snickers died. I could hear her in my head saying, "Oh sure. Leave it to Sheldon to die the day before I got all the attention. Stupid dog—always upstaging me."

Given the date, it made perfect sense, as I went through the motions that Thursday, that both Snickers and Sheldon visited me in amusing ways. When I arrived at my meeting at an area hotel, Snickers® candy bars were for sale on the counter. Only Snickers bars, no other candy of any kind. After the meeting I went into a consignment shop, where I found several used books by the author Sidney Sheldon. When I drove away from the shop, the nearby drug store had a digital sign out front reading "King Size Snickers $1.00!" My babies were visiting me everywhere.

When I got up Friday morning I was oddly euphoric. I felt like staying home, being alone to begin the process of writing Sheldon's story. I had been saying for years that I needed to tell his tale someday, even before I knew he had a chip that might unlock his mysteries.

My friend Annie, ever the researcher, had already investigated the names that the code from Sheldon's chip revealed. The Internet makes the task of mildly stalking someone doable right from home. The primary contact listed was a woman named Gabriela; a woman named Jackie was noted as an alternative contact. Annie gave me a call to tell me she hadn't discovered much on either of them, except that Gabriela was, or had been, a nanny. The search did not reveal more than that.

A few days after Sheldon died, I received his ashes. Bill, Lary, Bandit, and I gathered for our second pet memorial in twelve months. Unlike Snickers's tribute, which was held on a mild January afternoon, Sheldon's service took place on a frigid, sub-zero day. We all stood on my front porch, right where Sheldon perched when watching for kayakers, and spoke kind words about our sweet little guy.

Lary had given his words some serious thought. He said, "Sheldon was a particular dog. He was particular about what he ate and when he ate. He was particular about where he peed and pooped. He was also particular about guarding the river. But most of all, he was particular about who he chose as his caregiver and true companion. God Bless Sheldon and Tricia."

Sheldon had chosen me. He found me. He was considered a rescue dog, but I had also been rescued, simply because I loved him.

"Awww, thank you, Lary. That was beautiful." I was deeply touched by his words.

There was so much we could have said about Sheldon, but the bitter cold was driving us inside. Mere words seemed inadequate in expressing the loss we felt, and the bone-chilling temperature made our pain feel even more raw. All Bill could muster was, "He knows how I feel." With that, he went inside.

Lary and I scattered some of Sheldon's ashes. I spread some immediately off the porch steps, at S-man's favorite pee spot, right where the pee-on-mes grew each spring. Eventually, Sheldon's memorial marker would be placed in that very location. Lary took some ashes and followed Sheldon's path in the snow around the back of the house, scattering as he went. I dusted Sheldon's path at the front of the house. Remnants of Sheldon's earthly body were being returned to the hallowed ground, placed at optimum vantage points from which Sheldon's spirit could observe floaters and trains alike.

Before seeking the warmth of my riverside home, I stood a moment alone on the porch, pondering the life Sheldon had lived outside before joining me inside. There were many cold, dark, lonely nights endured in his quest to find me. His mission, his life's purpose, took him on a journey of perseverance I will never be able to truly appreciate but for which I am deeply and eternally grateful. Had it not been for a place called Rivershire, we'd never have been brought together. I speak of Sheldon and me rescuing each other. In truth, we were both rescued by Rivershire.

Give Me a Sign

When Wednesday rolled around, exactly one week after Sheldon's passing, the sadness overwhelmed me. I could not focus on anything. Tears were always in the corner of my eyes, threatening to tumble from their tenuous hold at any moment. I met Bill for a drink that afternoon around 5:00, but I was not good company. I stared across the bay through the pub's windows. I just needed to go home.

When I got to Rivershire, I paced around. Music, television, a movie, a bite to eat, nothing interested me. I needed to do something for Sheldon. I needed to write.

I brought out the yellow sheet of paper and studied it. I had not yet reached out to Gabriela; I was honestly unsure if I wanted to. What if she was angry with me for not having him scanned when I first took him to the veterinarian, so many years ago? What if she was nonchalant about what had happened to Sheldon? What if, like Shaun suspected, she had been abusive to him or abandoned him? I would be crushed to know Sheldon was deliberately mistreated.

I had only a phone number and an address for Gabriela. I knew one thing for sure in that moment: I could not call her. I wanted the words to be perfect and couldn't promise myself I would be capable of that by phone. I decided to write her a letter.

I sat at my computer, and the words flowed immediately and freely. I read it over. I changed nothing. I hit print. I was not convinced that I could send it, but it helped immensely to get the words out.

To: Gabriela XXXXXX

January 22, 2014

From: Tricia Frey

RE: My dog, Sheldon

Gabriela -

You and I have never met, but we have a connection. That connection comes in the form of an amazing, handsome, sweet and very, very special Blue Merle Sheltie whose name is Sheldon.

It's a long and fascinating story, but the short version is this: In the spring of 2006 I spotted a dog on my property on River Road in Traverse City, MI. At first, I thought he was a neighbor's dog but soon realized he was a stray. My sister and I made him a house, fed

*him daily, and began the journey of getting
him to trust us. He was so timid that it took
two years before I could even touch him for the
first time, and after a few pets and the removal
of the red collar he was wearing (there were no
tags), he took off into the woods again. And
so it went for the next six months. He'd come
close at times, allowing some petting, but then
he'd take off. Some times he'd be gone for a
couple weeks, then resurface again. Most of
the time he'd lurk on the fringe of the woods,
come and go from his house and keep an eye
on us. I can tell you, I fell in love even as he
kept his distance. And I named him Sheldon
early on. He had a home but had to decide to
trust me enough to come inside, and finally,
on October 11, 2008, he did. I immediately
dubbed October 11 Sheldon Day. Once inside,
it took a great deal of nurturing and patience,
but I gained his trust and we developed a bond
of love and adoration that I will treasure forever. Sadly, Sheldon passed away a week ago
today as a result of complications from an
enlarged heart. And with that, my heart shattered. I miss him terribly and am sure I will
for the rest of my life.*

*And so Sheldon's fascinating story contin-
ues. On the Sunday before his death, I took
him to the vet because he was vomiting and
not eating. X-rays were taken. Fluids and
anti-nausea shots were given and medication*

was prescribed. I took him home. The nausea ceased and he started eating again. By Tuesday, he was doing well. Then Wednesday, he took a turn for the worse. I took him to the vet and they stabilized him for a while, but he took a turn again and that afternoon he died in my arms.

And here's where you enter the story. When we took X-rays, we discovered that he had a microchip. Upon his death, I asked that he be scanned, hoping that maybe I could learn the rest of his story. The chip gave your name, address, and phone number as well as an alternate name of Jackie XXXXXX. It also indicated that he was a Sheltie Blue Merle, microchipped in 2003.

Please contact me via email. Sheldon meant the world to me and I deeply want to know his whole story. I can assure you he was loved, wanted, cared for, and adored by myself and many others. We all miss him deeply.

Thank you,

Tricia Frey

Writing the letter stirred up many emotions. As I lay in bed that night, I finally zoned in on what was really bothering me, on what was making me so very sad. What rose to the surface of my mind, plaguing me, was this: Is he all alone? Is he scared? Does he wonder where I am? I feared he may be wandering alone once again. I needed to know he was okay in the Great Beyond—for some reason, I was not sure. I prayed he was okay. A sign to help ease my heavy heart would be nice.

The next morning dawned crisp and cold, and my lingering sadness persisted. I showered, dressed, and headed to the rink. It was a magical winter's morning, and I found myself mesmerized by the sky. The color varied from a soft blue to steely gray, fringed on the horizon by a bright azure hue, interrupted occasionally by intermittent cloud cover. The sun was on the rise, hanging low in the sky, and a very light snow was falling. It was all incredibly serene.

What I saw as I pulled into the rink's parking lot stopped me in my tracks—literally. I locked up the car's brakes, skidding a bit before stopping abruptly. I threw the car into park and scrambled outside for a better look. The sun was breaking brightly through the gray, fully encircled by an even brighter ring, flanked on both sides by arcs that appeared to be a fragmented rainbow.

I called Becki, who was working inside the building. "Get out here! You've got to see this! There's a winter rainbow. It's unbelievable! Get out here!"

Becki walked over to the large windows overlooking the parking lot. "I can see it from here," she said. "Incredible!"

I hung up and took a few photos and a video. My video commentary went like this:

"Well it's hard to believe, but I pulled into the rink this morning, a gorgeous winter morning, one week and one day since the passing of my baby, and what do I see over the rink? Not only the sunshine but a rainbow, a winter rainbow. I see the two ends. I am, I am...I don't have words right now." But, apparently I did, because I continued: "Thank you, Sheldon, thank you. Best doggie ever! There's the rainbow bridge, baby. Go. Find Snickers. Play, romp, be happy. And when it's time for Mom to leave this world, we will meet on that bridge. I love you so much. Thank you. Be free. Romp happily. Play constantly. And love unconditionally, like you always have, and include yourself in that love, baby." Then I blew him a kiss.

I had my sign.

Sundogs
to the Rescue

I had rarely, if ever, experienced a winter rainbow, and I needed to investigate this spectacular phenomenon. Once I got inside, Becki and I began searching for answers. We discovered that what we had witnessed had a name: Sundogs. Yes, sundogs.

My research revealed a few definitions of sundogs, one of which particularly fit not only what Becki and I had seen, but described the author's real life dog in a Sheldon-like way. The account was by astronomer Richard Tresch Fienberg, and it read like this:

What is a sundog, or mock Sun? It's a concentrated patch of sunlight occasionally seen about 22° to the left or right of the Sun. Sundogs often form in pairs on either side of our daytime star, when sunlight refracts through icy clouds containing hexagonal platecrystals aligned with their large, flat faces parallel to the ground. Technically known as parhelia, singular parhelion, they are often white but sometimes quite colorful, looking like detached pieces of rainbow, with red on the inside, toward the Sun, and blue on the outside....

There are several authoritative books and websites about atmospheric phenomena, but none of the ones I checked say anything about why parhelia are called sundogs. My guess is their authors are cat people. I'm a dog person, and whenever I'm at home, my pooch, Duncan, follows me around the house close at my heels—just as a parhelion dogs the Sun. While I can't prove it, I'd wager the term "sundog" was coined by an observer with a dog. The term has been in use since the early 1600s, so we'll probably never know its origin for certain. (Richard Tresch Fienberg, Sky & Telescope, The Essential Guide to Astronomy)

I had my answer, my sign. Sheldon was not alone. Of course not. The one other dog with whom Sheldon connected most deeply had been waiting for him. Cousin Bowie found Sheldon and was leading his best cousin-buddy across the rainbow bridge as Becki and I watched together. I figured S-man was nipping at Bowie's heels all along the way.

As the sundogs in the sky faded, I recalled the letter tucked inside my briefcase. I handed it to

Becki. "Last night I wrote to Gabriela," I said. "I was a little vague and careful not to share too much. The way I wrote it gives the impression that I only discovered his chip this past weekend when he was sick. I don't want to be dishonest, but I'm being cautious with what I say because I have no idea how she'll react. I'm still deciding whether or not I should send it. Read it, and let me know what you think."

It didn't take Becki long to respond. "It's perfect. Don't change a word. Send it. Definitely send it."

Because I had left Gabriela's address at home on Thursday, I didn't mail it until Friday morning. As I pulled up to the mailbox I looked at the envelope one more time, finally deciding it was the right thing to do. I wanted answers. "Well, Sheldon, here it goes. Now, I'll just have to see if I ever get a response." With that, I dropped the letter in the slot.

I figured it was a long shot. After all, it was 2014; I first spotted Sheldon in 2006. People move, lives change. Gabriela might not live at the Franklin Park, Illinois, address any more. I expected to find the same envelope back in my own mailbox someday soon with the words "Return to Sender" stamped on the outside. All I could do now was to go on with my life and wait, which is exactly what I did.

I wouldn't have to wait for long.

Letters of Love

The weekend passed, and Monday was a busy day. As I was getting ready for bed I decided to check my emails. When the incoming mail loaded into my phone, five emails with the same words in the subject lines scrolled by. Each read "Sheldon the Sheltie."

I opened the first one.

On Jan 27, 2014, at 8:34 p.m., Gabriela wrote:

Hi Tricia! I just received your letter today and it made me cry! I am so glad I got to find out what happened to Riley. (That was what I had named him.)

Riley was born January 3, 2002, to a breeder in Canada. I got him when I was seventeen years old and he was a little eight-week-old puppy. He was going to be my agility buddy. He loved to stay by my side and was the sweetest boy, just like you described him.

I had two other Shelties as well. Faith was a

black tri-color and Bella was a Sable Sheltie. They were all the best of friends! I also had a Chow mix named Max and an Australian Shepherd.

I didn't know that our neighborhood allowed only two dogs per family. I was out in the front yard playing with the dogs when some-one from the community informed me of this. They said I had to place all but two of my dogs. It was the hardest decision I ever had to make! I chose to keep my first two dogs, Max and Faith. They both have since died.

I placed Riley with a lady in Michigan in 2006 who was looking for an agility partner. I felt she would provide a good home for Riley. His best friend, Bella, had previously left with another lady from North Carolina, and Riley was feeling a little down at having lost her. The lady from Michigan drove here to meet Riley and he did great with her. It broke my heart when she put him in her truck and drove away. Riley was staring through the window at me, so sad and desperate to get back to me. I knew he would have a good home with her and that, no matter how much I wanted to, I couldn't keep him.

About a week after she had gotten Riley, I received an email from her saying she was devastated. She had been walking with Riley in a field without his leash. Something spooked him and he ran off into the woods. I was heartbroken, thinking the worst, and that Riley had probably run off to try and find me. I blamed myself for him being lost.

The lady put up fliers and went searching through the woods for him for months. Every time she updated me that she hadn't found him, my heart would break all over again. I believed that Riley had been killed by some wildlife and that I was to blame for his fate. I never stopped thinking about him. I knew he had the microchip, which is why I held out hope that if he was ever found I would be notified.

I am so happy that Riley/Sheldon found such an amazing home with a caring person like you, who never gave up on him, and was patient enough to win his trust and love. I am glad that he lived a happy life with you where he was taken care of and loved. I can never thank you enough for this closure and for being so good to Riley/Sheldon.

I will email pictures so you can see him when he lived here with me and my family. We loved him as well.

Thanks again and God bless you for your kindness to Riley. Knowing he was loved has made me so happy just now.

Gabby

The four emails that followed all contained photos showing Riley/Sheldon at different stages in his life with Gabby; puppy and young adult, sometimes by himself, but also with his former best canine buddies, two of whom were now also waiting for him across the rainbow bridge. He was not alone—far from it.

I had two favorite photos from the mix. One showed all five dogs gathered together on the lawn. Another was an extreme close-up of Sheldon looking right into the camera, wearing a tag that clearly read, "Gabby Loves Riley." Elation and heartbreak surged through me simultaneously.

Sheldon was not abused. He was loved. He was missed. I was thrilled to know this, to connect the dots. I was also heartbroken about what he had gone through. Taken from the only home he had ever known—away from people and other dogs he loved dearly, driven to a place he'd never been with a total stranger—must have caused Sheldon, such a timid and tender-hearted dog, great anxiety. I envisioned him looking out that window at Gabby as he was driven away. I could not help but cry.

What was done, however, was done. Sheldon had good things happen to him since getting lost. He knew the meaning of home and love—and even trust—once again. And, as a result of Sheldon's suffering, I more fully comprehended their meanings as well.

Although Gabby had sent the emails earlier in the evening, it was nearly 11:00 p.m. when I saw them. Too late to call anyone with this exciting development—which was just fine. In that moment the knowledge was all mine, and I wanted to revel in it by myself. I was so grateful to Gabby; overwhelmed with the love, kindness, and revealing honesty with which she shared her story. If I could have, I would have stretched my arms through those emails all the way to Franklin Park, Illinois, and hugged her long and hard.

The last email to come in from Gabby that evening said this:

> *Tricia, I wanted to let you know that I also forwarded your email to the lady who got Riley. Her name is Nancy and she is so happy and relieved that he found such a great home. She asked me if it's okay if she contacts you as well?*
>
> *Gabby*

Of course I wanted to connect with Nancy, too. I got an email from her the next morning with additional details. I discovered there was a bit of a twist to the story. Isn't there always?

> *January 28, 10:46 a.m.*
>
> *Hi Tricia,*
>
> *My name is Nancy. I live in Kingsley and purchased Riley from Gabby several years ago. I got Riley because I enjoyed competing in agility. I wanted a small dog to work with and he sounded like he would fit the bill.*

I think Gabby may have already told you, Riley and I were in an accident and he got loose. We were coming home one evening after dark and a car passed me on Walton Road near Summit City Road. It hit black ice and spun out of control, hitting us. When the car door was opened, Riley took off.

I made up fliers and passed them out everywhere. I contacted Animal Control, rescue groups, and shelters. I put advertisements in the paper and posted fliers everywhere I could think of. I mailed fliers out to veterinarian offices. I knew he had a microchip and, if someone brought in a dog matching his description, I wanted the vets to check for a chip. I borrowed snowshoes and went into the woods searching for him and drove the roads looking for him every opportunity I had. I finally figured that the worst had happened to him and that I would not find him. I was in touch with Gabby because she was still the contact person for his microchip.

Riley was very shy so I took him with me everywhere, introducing him to many different things, and working on a bond with him. He slept in bed with me along with a couple other canines. I am sure you can imagine the trauma he experienced in the accident and how that would add to his already existing fears.

When I read your letter that Gabby shared with me, I could not hold back the tears. It is so good to know that he was found, cared for, and loved. There is some closure in knowing that he shared a good, loving home for many years. He traveled a long distance to get to you. He really was a survivor.

Thank you, Tricia, for caring for Riley who deserved so much. I know he gave love back to you. God bless you for sharing your life with a very special little guy.

Sincerely,

Nancy

It touched me that Nancy also referred to Sheldon as "little guy," those same sweet words that Bill repeated the night he died. He was a special little guy indeed.

I replied to both Gabby and Nancy. Several emails circulated between the three of us, and some details didn't completely jibe. Initially, Gabby said that Sheldon ran off when Nancy was walking him off-leash about a week after Nancy took him to northern Michigan. Then, Nancy wrote that a car accident resulted in his running away, later informing me Sheldon had been with her for about six weeks. No one attempted to fabricate the details. For whatever reason, their stories of how Sheldon had gotten lost varied. Time had passed, causing memories of the details to fade and distort. I never doubted there was a car accident. Nancy's account of that night was very vivid and rang true. It also helped explain Sheldon's overall anxiety, especially where car rides were concerned.

What mattered was that Sheldon found his way to northern Michigan—and eventually to Rivershire—where he wandered his way into the hearts of many new people who came to love him as deeply as those who had been lost to him. When I shared the story with my niece Lori and her husband, Jon, she texted me back these words: "Jon's mouth is hanging open. I cannot stop crying. He was always loved."

Indeed he was.

One Year Later
01/15/2015

Exactly one year after Sheldon left this earth, he visited me in the form of a prism of light. It appeared across a Christmas card sent to me by my friend Cindy. On the front of the card was a picture of a polar bear in white, gray, and silver tones, much like Sheldon. The words on the cover of the card, Wonder and Joy, were soothing to me. I was not yet ready to dispose of the card, so I moved it to a new, special spot on the shelf, where it was surrounded by photos of Sheldon—including a picture of him and me together—and other treasures connected to people dear to me. As soon as I placed it there, a rainbow spectrum appeared on the card, created by light passing through a cut glass bowl on the shelf above. "Hello Sheldon, there you are. I knew you would visit today." He stayed close all day long.

An Amaizin' Visit

In the spring of 2017 I took a two-week road trip to visit my dear friend, Lou, in Cleveland, Tennessee. The trip included Ohio stops on the way there and back. I also added an important side trip into the Carolinas. I had long wanted to visit Asheville, North Carolina, and from there I headed to the Charlotte area, as Gabby had previously shared with me that Sheldon's best buddy, Bella, went to live with a woman named Charlotte from that region. At the time of my initial correspondence with Gabby, Bella was still alive, living on a farm with Charlotte and her husband, Tommy.

However, by the time I took my road trip Bella had passed. I could imagine her and Sheldon reunited and romping freely together once again. That comforting thought made me want to meet Charlotte even more. I knew she had started breeding Shelties since acquiring Bella, and I thought maybe I could meet some of Bella's bloodline. But mostly, I had this deep need to meet Charlotte and experience her farm. I was not exactly sure why.

I contacted her and briefly explained how I had come to know about her. Initially, she assumed I might want to come look at puppies to adopt, but I explained that no, I simply wanted to visit. She agreed.

Charlotte and I had a very special visit on her farm. While I was there, Sheldon came to me in the form of a very small, sweet Australian Shepherd.

Although not a Sheltie, this dog reminded me of Sheldon because of her markings and attitude. She immediately approached and sniffed my leg but did not seem completely sure of me. I sensed she would like to herd me. Instead, she stayed close and let me pet her. "Who is this little sweetie?" I asked Charlotte. "That's Maisey," she replied. Of course that was her name. Although spelled differently, all I heard was Maize, as in Maize and Blue—as in Sheldon, the Amaizin' Blue Wonder Dog.

Charlotte and I sat and talked in the horse barn for an hour and a half. I met her family of delightful dogs, some bred by her and Tommy—including a couple in Bella's line—and others who had been rescued. Maisey was a rescue and, like Sheldon, she too had an incredible story of becoming lost and—after a long, hard journey—returning home to the farm where she was dearly loved and missed. Maisey's story, as I recall it, involved her traveling with Charlotte and Tommy to a horse show during which Maisey had run off and become lost. Word was circulated in the area and locals would report sightings of the frightened little dog, but, like with Sheldon, no one could get near her. Then, some folks realized that Maisey was hiding in a shed on their property. They closed Maisey inside and Tommy came to get her. Tommy found a terrified Maisey cowering in a dark corner, unwilling to emerge—that is, until Tommy spoke. Maisey heard a voice she knew and loved and she ran to Tommy, jumping into his waiting arms. It was an emotional and joyful reunion.

While Charlotte and I visited, Maisey stayed nearby, except for the time she got up and began nipping at the heels of a horse in the corral who clearly, in Maisey's opinion, needed herding. Huge in size compared to tiny Maisey, the horse's enormity didn't concern Maisey. There was a job to be done. Charlotte instructed Maisey to leave the horse alone and, finally, with definite reluctance, Maisey returned to relax with us. There was an intensely familiar presence with me in the barn that day.

Charlotte related emotionally to the story I shared about Sheldon. She held a tiny Sheltie, with a few more gathered around her feet, the entire time we spoke. For the duration of the story she wiped her eyes as the tears flowed. My sharing of the discovery of Sheldon's microchip provided an especially heart-wrenching moment. Charlotte completely grasped the intense torment that revelation had caused me. She also assured me I had done the right thing for Sheldon by not contacting his previous caregivers prior to his passing. Not knowing if they would have wanted him back, secrecy until his death was the only choice I could have made. Charlotte knew a great deal about Shelties and, on the day of our visit, I received an important lesson in Sheltie Behavior 101.

I knew Sheldon was sensitive, but I didn't fully comprehend how sensitive the breed is as a whole. As I learned from Charlotte, the sensitive Sheltie bonds very deeply to his caretakers—more so than most other dog breeds—and is committed to remaining together for life's duration. When a Sheltie is separated or removed from his home and the people he loves, he takes it very personally, internalizing that the separation is his fault. It takes a Sheltie a long time to bond with different people, if it ever truly happens. Even a Sheltie's natural instinct to herd can become suppressed; distrust, timidity, and fear overrule. The displaced Sheltie becomes withdrawn, even more skittish and timid than is normal for the breed. Trusting anyone again takes a very long time, and the humans involved must possess a great deal of patience and dedication.

Learning more about Sheltie behavior in general revealed a lot to me about Sheldon and the process we both traversed in helping him to trust me. First, he was removed from his home, and he felt the separation was his fault. Then, a terrifying car accident accelerated his fear and distrust. He was traumatized by all that had happened to him. It took years for him to fully know and trust me, and when that finally occurred, his personality and natural instincts were able to emerge once again.

When I left the farm, my newfound understanding about a Sheltie's personality gave me peace. I had answers as to why it took Sheldon over two years to come inside. I understood why his behavior changed from withdrawn doggie to herding maniac. I was deeply comforted. Plus, Sheldon's visit in the physical form of Maisey overwhelmed me with love, joy, and sheer awe. Sheldon was with me always, and his presence that day in the barn was particularly intense. I drove away from Charlotte's farm, traveling down that county road, knowing exactly what had compelled me to visit. I needed answers about Sheldon, and I received them where his best friend, Bella, once lived. Leave it to a couple of Shelties to herd me exactly where I needed to go.

In Sheldon's Words

"All in all, I had a very good life. There was, of course, that period of two to three years where things got pretty rough, but I had some good times then, too, and I found my true earthly home. I was meant to be at Rivershire with Tricia from the minute I was born. It took a special kind of journey to get there.

I was lucky enough to have three human moms, and I was always loved. That's more than a lot of critters and people can say. My first mom, other than my canine birth mom, was Gabby, and she loved me a lot. She even made me a special tag for my collar that read: "Riley—Loved by Gabby." Riley was my first name. Gabby made the right decision when she gave me up to my second mom, Nancy, although I did not understand it at the time. All I knew then was that I was being taken away from the only home and mom I had ever known. I'd already had my heart broken when my best friend, Bella, left. Then, I was driven away in a truck with someone I did not know. I watched out the back window as Gabby disappeared from my life, and it hurt terribly. I was scared, confused, and sad.

But the ride with Nancy, my new mom, was a necessary part of the journey to my true home. Nancy was wonderful, and she loved me right away. She took very good care of me, showing me love and understanding; she wanted me to trust and love her in turn, and I started to do so. I could have been very happy with her, but that was not meant to be.

The car accident shattered my world. I was already timid by nature, just starting to adapt to my new home and accept the love of a new mom, but I still had trust issues. So much had changed in such a short period of time. I missed my first home, my mom and friends, and was trying to accept what was happening to me. Then, a horrible, scary accident happened. I was terrified. When the car door opened, I ran. And I ran. And I ran. I never saw Nancy or my second home again.

I had no idea where I was going. I traveled 10 miles in about two months, finding food and shelter along the way wherever I could. It was hard. It was winter. There was snow and ice. I was cold, and so very afraid. I was chased, shot at, and saw other animals that wanted to attack me, each experience more deeply ingraining my traits of skittishness and timidity. I was terrified and could not trust anyone. That's why, when I saw Tricia for the first time through the window at Rivershire, I fled.

By now, you know the story. I not only learned to trust Tricia, but I adored her on an elevated level born of the hardships I endured. She became my true protector and I became hers. Our devotion to each other ran deep, offering immeasurable rewards to two lives in need of resuscitation. A bond like that can never be severed.

Now, I romp happily and freely with all my friends that passed before me. Snickers, Gracie, and I watch out for Mom and visit her frequently from beyond the realm of the earthly world. She senses us. She talks to us. She continues to love us and will never stop. I did not know all of Mom's other pets that came before me, but I know she carries them in her heart, too.

We wait for Mom. She still needs to be on earth for reasons we do not know. Maybe it's because she needs to tell our story, to complete our journey, hers included. When it's her time to leave earth, we will be waiting with open paws. We will come running. We will jump on her and cover her with kisses. She will hug and pet us. We will roam and explore together.

I learned a lot in my twelve years on Earth. Life can be hard at times. Things do not always make sense. Sometimes, it seems that everything is going wrong. Yet, I found courage and my way in this world. When I least expected it, I found a beautiful home at Rivershire, making all the pain worthwhile. I would encourage you to ask yourself, especially when life is rough, "What miraculous thing might happen to me today?" Delightful surprises and blessings await us all.

Here's some advice from a once-wayward dog. Trust in goodness. Offer and accept love. Embrace life and give the best of yourself, whatever you can muster. We do not have to move mountains to shake up the Universe. Be brave. Persevere. And, perhaps most importantly, herd when you have to.

Love, Sheldon"

Epilogue:
Happy Sheldon Day

"It's Happy Sheldon Day, the second one since Sheldon's passing. Since then, I, Bandit, have been the sole Rivershire dog, left to roam the property along with the chipmunks, birds, otters, beavers, deer, raccoons, martens, and occasional bear.

I've had my struggles since Sheldon left. My heart and soul want to play and swim like I used to, but my body simply says 'no.' My hips are shot; I can't leap into the air to snatch a flippy no matter how strong my desire. If I were to try, I would collapse hard to the ground as soon as gravity did its job. These old hips wouldn't stick the landing, not a chance.

I can't hear worth a damn. If someone is standing near me and wants to get my attention, they have to touch me. My eyesight is failing, too. I'm old, and I'm ready to go. My dad Lary, however, isn't quite there. He's not unaware that my days are numbered, it's just that he can't quite bring himself to make the call. It's hard for humans to put us out of our misery, even when they know it's for the best, that we're ready. I've been ready for a while. I'm in pain. I ache all over, and my joints throb. I'm so very ready.

Tonight, I wait for Dad to come home. It feels like a long time since he left and it is very dark outside. I don't hear him when he comes in. I'm sound asleep by the front door waiting, but I don't realize he is home until he touches me to let me know he's there. This makes me happy. Seeing Dad always makes me happy.

But, first things first. I have to pee. As always, Dad lets me out the sliding door to do my business and, as soon as I've relieved myself, I go back in to get my treats and lots of loving. My dad has had me since I was a puppy, and we are best friends. I love to get lots of loving from Dad.

After receiving loving and treats from Dad, I head out the door again. I don't require a leash and haven't for many, many years. I am well-trained, but more than this, I am smart and loyal. I understand my boundaries and want to be near home and Dad. I enjoy taking my nightly loop around Rivershire. Dad stays inside and relaxes, grabs himself a beer while

I do this. I always return to the door when I've had enough of a fresh air stroll for the night. Then, it's time for dinner. I don't like to eat when Dad's gone. I wait for him to get home. When I get back to the door, I will go in and clean up the kibble waiting in my bowl.

But no, not tonight. I start my stroll around the property and feel the old, dull ache in my hips and bones sink in deeper. Winter is coming. It's getting colder. The pain will only get worse. Tonight is beautiful. The stars are out, and the moon is a bright sliver in the sky. The air is still warm enough and we're having a lovely, mild fall. As I saunter my way closer to the bank I feel the river's pull. It smells so inviting. The cool water would feel very good on my painful hips. It would be so nice to take one more swim. The buoyancy of the water would take the weight off my throbbing joints. I want that relief. I need that relief.

It's time. I want to rid Dad of the decision. I got my treats and loving. I said my goodbye. I want to swim again like I used to. I want to swim to the next life. I'm a big dog. I can make this decision, and I will so that Dad doesn't have to.

As I enter the water, I'm as excited as a puppy again. The cool water feels so good on my aching body. My legs know just what to do, but instead of going upstream to wait for the flippy, then swimming it back to Dad,

I'm just going to take a nice, leisurely swim downstream. The stars are out overhead, and the sliver of the brilliant moon is ahead of me, guiding me. I start to paddle, but it's not necessary. The river is taking me, and all I have to do is steer a bit. Yes, the river knows. The river is my path to the next life.

I sense that people are looking for me. There are light beams dancing in the night, flashlights. I've always loved chasing flashlight beams, but not tonight. I have somewhere else to be. I even think I hear Dad and Tricia calling—but, they know better. I'm deaf as a stone after all. But, I do hear something. I hear the river and, yes, YES! I hear barking! Sheldon is waiting, beckoning me to come to a better place, one without pain, one where flippies fly freely and a dog can swim and retrieve toys forever. As I swim, I start to rise. I can see Sheldon now—he has a big Golden Retriever and some other friends with him, including that cat that hissed at me when I smelled her butt. I believe her name is Snickers. Goodbye, Dad. Goodbye, Rivershire. I'll be watching from beyond, and I'll never, ever stray far from you."

On Sunday, November 1, 2015, three weeks after Bandit took his final swim, Lary got a call from a neighbor downstream. Bandit's body had surfaced at his property and was caught in some felled branches. Lary retrieved Bandit from the neighbor who had kindly pulled Bandit from the river and laid him on his lawn. The cold water had done a nice job of preserving Bandit, and Lary lovingly wrapped him in a blanket and brought him home. Lary dug a grave in the scrub at the edge of Garden of Grace, where Bandit was laid to rest with a proper memorial. Lary and I spoke words of love, relief, and gratitude. Rivershire's powerful and magical magnetic force would not be denied. Exactly as was meant to be, all God's children were home.

The End

MATT LOWER

BARBIE STERLING

Acknowledgements

Writing *River Love* has been a true labor of love. It took me six years to get to the publishing phase. Everything in its right time.

A lot can happen in six years, but one very significant thing occurred just this year, on February 3, 2020. Ronnie, a significant part of the *River Love* story, passed away suddenly and unexpectedly from an apparent heart attack. Our world crumbled a bit that day, but Ronnie's spirit held us up. I can see him now, in the Great Beyond, Bowie and Sheldon by his side. Ronnie, thank you for loving my sister with your whole heart. Thank you for being another big brother to me. And, thank you for being a part of our lives. We will love and miss you forever.

I have many people to thank for the help, love, and encouragement they extended to me during the writing and publishing of *River Love*. I am deeply grateful to the following:

To my very first readers, Sandra and Becki. They both plodded through a long, rough manuscript with confusing tense changes and an array of other issues. They made suggestions as to what content should stay, go, or be revised. I went back in and cut over 40,000 words and corrected the tense. Becki agreed to read it again. Sandra dove back in and provided expert advice and copy editing tasks that helped me with yet more revising. Through the process, Sandra helped me identify and draw out pieces of myself I needed to address and share to make the story complete. That early help, encouragement, and honest feedback from both was vital in getting the manuscript from rough draft to the final editing process. Having sisters involved in this arduous and deeply personal process could have been risky; instead, it was beautiful, and richer sisterhood developed because of it.

To my first professional reviewer, John Pahl, who pinpointed key areas of the manuscript that needed attention, revision and, most importantly, further exploration. His initial assessment provided an expert nudge that sent *River Love* flowing in the right direction.

To my line editor, Scott Couturier, whose expertise, wisdom, talent, and huge heart helped navigate the manuscript to a place of honest revelation and properly honed narrative. Through our collaboration, he became a trusted guide and, more importantly, a trusted friend.

To my copy editor, Darlene Short, whose brilliance, professionalism, ability to embrace tedium, and project dedication made the copy editing process a breeze for me. She took the full weight of it and handled it with amazing skill. Darlene and I went to school together, K-12. We played together at my house and her mom took us to see *Herbie the Love Bug*. Through this collaboration, our younger selves became acquainted with our adult selves, and I am richer for the experience. Darlene's authentic, kind and spirited nature warms me to the core. Should I need a copy editor again in the future, I will always look to Darlene, my talented and trustworthy friend.

To Barbie Sterling, whose amazing artistic and photographic talents visually bring Sheldon to life for the reader. Barbie and I are longtime friends and there was no one else I wanted to design the *River Love* cover. The design process was involved and challenging at times—made more difficult by the inability to work together in the same space due to the COVID pandemic—yet fun and incredibly rewarding. Barbie knew and loved Sheldon and is a dedicated animal lover and rescuer. Connecting in these ways and more, we are kindred spirits.

To Bill, my wonderful companion, for believing I could bring this story to life. Every time I started to doubt I would ever finish the book, I'd remember him saying, "If there's anyone I know that can write a book, it's you. I know you can do it." Simple words of encouragement go a long way, especially when they come from someone you love.

To Gabriela and Nancy, Sheldon's first moms,

for responding with such an outpouring of love and comfort when they learned what had happened to the dog formerly known as Riley. The compassion and love they had for Sheldon was evident in every word of their beautiful letters. He was always loved, indeed.

To friends and family members who, taking time to read *River Love* in its various stages, offered encouragement and feedback along the way. I appreciate this gesture more than they will ever know.

To Dr. Richard Tresch Fienberg, Press Officer of the Astronomical Society, and the Crew at StoryPeople, for granting me permission to use their quotes and material in this story. *River Love* would have lacked something special without the inclusion of their insights.

To Susan Vants, Kathy Partin, Matt Lower and Barbie Sterling for allowing me to include their wonderful photos of Sheldon and me. Kathy came to Rivershire one lovely day during the COVID pandemic and took riverside photos of me from a socially safe distance. These are special people in my life and it is an honor to share their talents within these pages.

To the professionals at Mission Point Press—especially Anne Stanton, Doug Weaver, Heather Shaw and Jodee Taylor—for all their help and support. The task of publishing was daunting to me, especially as a first-time author. I didn't want to lose creative control of this personal project, but I didn't have the publishing expertise to see it

SUSAN VANTS, LIL RED'S PHOTOGRAPHY

through to fruition without a great deal of trial and error. The partnership with MPP provided both collaboration and expert assistance, the perfect combination for me.

Finally, I am eternally and deeply grateful to the Universe for drawing me, my sisters and Sheldon to this slice of paradise called Rivershire. I owe a great deal to this special place, and yet it asks for nothing in return. One day, while pondering all that had occurred to bring Sheldon and me together at Rivershire, an adage came to mind—Bravely go to that place where you are meant to be. I wish this for you, too, dear reader.

Bravely go....

Peace and Gratitude,
Tricia

KATHLEEN S. PARTIN

Tricia Frey was raised on a farm in Northwest Ohio where her love of animals began. Over the years, pets in need of rescue—several cats and one wayward Sheltie—found their way into her home and heart. Early on, Tricia developed a love of reading and writing that she continued to pursue throughout her high school and college years. Culminating in a Bachelor of Arts degree in Public Relations and Professional Writing from Capital University, Columbus, Ohio, Tricia has since made a career in sales and marketing. Her love of Northern Michigan brought her to Traverse City in the late 1990's, where she now lives at her beloved Rivershire, nestled on the banks of the Boardman River. Tricia spends her free time nurturing her gardens, walking the many nearby beaches and hiking trails, and kayaking the beautiful Boardman.

Readers are encouraged to visit www.triciafrey.com to contact the author for speaking engagements or to get information on how to buy this book in bulk at a discounted rate.

This photo of Sheldon was taken approximately two years after he was seen for the first time at Rivershire while he was still living outside. He had become woolly and matted. Soon after the photo was taken, Tricia was able to begin trimming off clumps of matted fur as Sheldon would allow. Summer of 2008. Photographer unknown.

In memory of Ronnie Van Horn

Made in the USA
Monee, IL
15 October 2020

45084635R00163